AND THERE WOULD BE NO WOLVES

"And There Would Be No Wolves," by Leatrice Lifshitz. ISBN 978-1-60264-080-1.

Published 2007 by Virtualbookworm.com Publishing Inc., P.O. Box 9949, College Station, TX 77842, US.

Manufactured in the United States of America.

CHAPTER 1

MY NAME IS MARY BROWN. I want you to know it. To say it. To remember it whenever you hear someone say John Brown. Mary. Mary Brown. Mary Anne Brown.

Not that I want to blaspheme. I know it was God's will. And I know the Lord works in mysterious and wondrous ways. But now that it's over, I want to be remembered, to be connected to what my life was—the life that was given to me, slowly, day after day, and yet somehow suddenly. Just a woman's life. Nothing fancy. Nothing big. But where would John Brown have been without his sons? Without my sons? Where would John Brown have been without Mary Brown's sons?

It is a simple story.

A man came, cleared the land and built a house. It was a fine house—a two story log house with two fireplaces, one at either end. I remember even as a child some days I could see the smoke rising from the chimneys—so far apart, the smoke just rose up separately into the sky. For a long time. All the years I was growing up, I remember that. The smoke.

Also the man. But then, who didn't know John Brown? Who didn't admire him?

It seemed there was nothing that John Brown didn't know. Well, I suppose some of the time he was still searching, but at least he knew what he was searching for. He knew what it was he needed to know. He knew what everyone needed: truth and faith. And he was strong in that. I mean he was a grown man but he still studied it. He read books about it. And if it happened that you asked him something he wasn't exactly sure of, he would look it up in one of his books. And if you doubted him, he would show it to you as plain as the nose on your face.

"A book is the extra pair of shoes on the long hard road to righteousness," he said. "A book is the turnkey in Heaven's door."

Yes, John Brown knew everything that needed knowing, and he could do anything that needed to be done. Anything. It was true, he was a big, strong man and he could plow a field as well as anyone, but he could also bake a loaf of bread or sing a lullaby. Everyone knew it. Of course, after we married he didn't have to do those woman chores, but that's a longer leap than I should be telling.

It was cold. I think it was cold. The sun just coming up, but the trees still holding the darkness of the night. I took the path my sister had taken a few weeks before. To the edge of town, through the forest, past the corner of a small cornfield, staying away from the village of the Indian peoples, the long low houses that crowded and tumbled one into another.

"Cross the stream by the hemlock grove," my sister had told me. "The stream is tighter there, with a few well-placed, flat-topped stones. Then turn left. And follow the smoke."

I was young and strong. I liked being out of the house and I walked quickly. But after a while my feet were wet with snow and my hands were cold, almost numb. Once or twice I had to stop to stamp my feet and I blew on my fingers to warm them.

It seemed like the morning was half over when I found the hemlock grove. Then I crossed the stream and turned left. In a little ways I came out of the forest. Wolves were howling. Maybe it was an omen. Maybe not. Wolves howled a lot and I didn't think too much about it. What I noticed was that the shadows were now behind me and the way in front of me was clear. It was easy, like being in a meadow. I clenched my hand into a fist to feel my fingers, to warm them. My right hand. My left hand. Open and close. Open and close. Then, looking up, just as my sister had said, there was the smoke. And I followed it.

CHAPTER 2

I CAME TO SPIN.

My sister cooked and cleaned and did the wash. I spun. Flax and wool. For clothes and sheets and blankets. For five children without a mother. And for their father, John Brown.

Those days. Were they happy? I don't think anyone thought about being happy. I never once heard that word. Ever. Maybe I wasn't smart enough. Maybe I was too young. But I don't think my sister thought about being happy either. On those cold winter days, she was the first one up in the morning to light the fire and the last one in bed at night. There was no time to think about being happy. There was no time to think. There were only two times: praying time and working time. Churn the butter, cook the corn meal, feed the family and tend to the animals. But it's also true that time, without even thinking about it, can get away from you like a bubble. A little time to plan—or dream.

"When I am married, you can stay here if you wish," my sister said one evening as I left the large spinning wheel by the fire and we climbed the stairs to bed. She started to undress. "You know there will be more children and more work," she added.

I smiled. "Mrs. Brown," I said softly.

She smiled. "Mrs. Brown," she said.

Of course, that wasn't quite right. People still talked about Mrs. Brown. The first Mrs. Brown. Dianthe Brown.

Wolves bothered her, people said. And noise and dirt and smoke—hiding from them as much as she could. Watching her children. Guarding them. Teaching them. One. Two. Three. Four. Five. Six. Year after year. Six children and then Frederick caught the fever and died.

Did she forget to hoe her garden? Did she serve porridge for dinner, cabbage for breakfast? Did she break a dish or two?

She was confused, some people said. She was crazy, some people said. She was tired, some people said.

She liked the quiet of a forest. She liked the comfort of a hymn. She sang to her husband. She sang to her children. She sang to the journeymen who worked in her husband's tannery. She sang to herself.

Blow ye the trumpet, blow
Sweet is Thy work, my God, my King.
I'll praise my Maker with my breath.
O, happy is the man who hears.
Why should we start, and fear to die.
With songs and honors sounding loud.
Ah, lovely appearance of death.

And more babies. Two more babies, the last one dying before he could suckle.

"It's not your fault," the doctor said.

He took the baby from her. Then he felt her forehead. He listened to her heart. He held her hand. He shook his head.

"Mrs. Brown," he asked, "are you afraid?"

Dianthe shivered. Her hands twisted around each other, but she took a deep breath and her voice was calm.

"No, sir," she said. "Why should I be afraid? It is the Sabbath and it always pleased me to think I might go to rest on God's Sabbath."

Then Dianthe raised herself on one elbow, pulled the blanket up to her shoulders and turned to her husband.

"I want to see the children," she said.

And they came.

John, Jr. who was eleven. Jason who was nine and a half. And Owen who was almost seven.

"Say it with me," she said.

And she began.

The Lord is my shepherd, I shall not want.
He maketh me to lie down in green pastures.
He restoreth my soul.
He leads me in the paths of righteousness for His name's sake.
Yea, though I walk through the valley of the shadow of death, I will fear no evil; for You are with me; Your rod and Your staff, they comfort me.
You prepare a table before me in the presence of my enemies; You anoint my head with oil; my cup runneth over.
Surely goodness and mercy shall follow me all the days of my life; and I shall dwell in the house of the Lord forever.

When they were finished, John, Jr. came close to hug her. Jason was breathing hard and gulping air. Owen started to cry. But Dianthe, looking at each child, just said, "Love is love. Love is always love and we will meet again in our Eternal Home."

Then the two little ones came. Ruth who was three and a half and the second Frederick who was one and a half. Dianthe waved them to her bed.

Her voice was soft, but sweet, and she sang.

Why should we start, and fear to die.
With songs and honors sounding loud.
Ah, lovely appearance of death.

And then the children were taken away. Her children. The children my sister thought would be hers.

But that's not the way it would be. Not the way it was meant to be. I don't know why. I never asked and I was never told. I don't think it was something I did or didn't do. It just happened. In the spring.

My sister had cooked a fine meal of corn bread, beef stew and pumpkin pudding. When we finished eating, she got up to clear the table and I started for the loom, to finish the cloth I was weaving.

Mr. Brown... I was still calling him Mr. Brown then, didn't say anything. He just stood in front of me, blocking my way. He didn't touch me. He just pointed to a piece of paper he was putting on the edge of the table.

"Read it," he said, "I await your answer."

My heart was racing. I had never been so close to Mr. Brown before. And I don't think he ever spoke to me directly.

"Read it."

What was it? Was he angry because the cloth was not yet done? Was he angry because his shirt sleeve was too long? Was he angry because I spilled the soup when I was passing it?

"I await your answer."

No, it was something he wanted me to tell him. What? What could John Brown want me to tell him?

Once again my sister and I climbed the stairs together. I held the note against my heart. When I undressed, I felt awkward. My clothes came off slowly. My hair fell down slowly. I slipped the note beneath my pillow. I turned from my sister and said nothing.

Like God's own hand, that night stretched into darkness and deepness. I fell into the dreams that came and then slipped away. But I remembered one dream. It was a warm day and I was sitting on a cushion, floating, gently floating, almost as if I had wings. Then, just as I was going to land, I saw that my cushion was nothing more than a plain piece of paper. I was worried but there was nothing I could do, and when I landed my cushion was torn into small pieces. I started to gather the pieces together as fast as I could but then a wind came up, and suddenly there were many people, all grabbing for a piece of paper. I remember it so clearly–it just seemed that hands were everywhere. Grabbing hands. And then it began to snow. Imagine snow on such a warm day!

After that I awoke and saw that the bedclothes had come undone and my feet were twitching with the morning's cold. I almost smiled at how my feet had walked themselves into my dream, but I had overslept and I hurried to get dressed. Then I remembered the note beneath my pillow. It was time to know what was in it.

CHAPTER 3

I WALKED TOWARD THE WELL.

"I am just Mary Anne Day," I kept saying to myself. "I am just Mary Anne Day and he is John Brown."

Round and round in my head, that's all I said, all I thought of. But I could feel the note in my pocket. It was getting heavy, like a stone. And then I had a different feeling, that I was like a pond and the stone was sinking into me. And there was no sound. No splash. No ripple.

I did not hurry. I took the long way to the well, up the rise from the tannery, to the side of the barn. Lily of the Valley were blooming early, everywhere, even as I walked further on past Dianthe's grave. And, of course, the little birds, the yellow ones, were hopping all over the trees: birch and oak and maple.

I reached the well and lowered my bucket down into it. A full day time moon was shimmering in it.

"I am just Mary Anne Day. I am just Mary Anne Day."

The bucket was full and I slowly hauled it up, lifted it to my hip and turned to go. There was a breeze and I pulled my shawl closer around my shoulders, feeling its warmth and wondering what it would be like to have a ribbon in my hair. What color? Red? White? Black?

Idle thoughts, I knew, and I walked quickly as if to leave them behind. I heard the water slosh in the bucket, saw some of it spill out and darken the side of my skirt. "First idle, then clumsy," I said to myself, glad that there was no one to see me. Then a shadow by the fence post began to move. It got taller and wider as it came closer. It came very close and stopped directly in front of me. It was John Brown.

I looked at him, once, only once, and then looked away. Scared? I wasn't exactly scared and I wasn't exactly not scared. I was looking. I was searching. I was wanting a sign, that's what it was. I was wishing for a sign to tell me yes or no. But there was no sign, except for one of those little yellow birds that began to sing into the silence.

"Yes, sir," I said. "Yes."

I stood there, thinking I should say something else, something more, maybe tell him something about myself, but I couldn't think of anything. I shuffled my feet in the mud. I pulled my shawl tighter around my shoulders.

"Yes, sir," I said again. "Yes."

"Good," he said. "I will make the arrangements."

And I followed him up the path till he turned to the tannery and I turned to the house. Looked at it. The garden. The orchard. The barn. The slope to the brook beyond the tannery. The path the men made walking from the tannery to the house and from the house to the tannery. Even the clothes drying on the line. The same clothes as last week and the week before. The same colors.

Carefully, longer than I needed to, I wiped the mud from my boots. My heart was neither heavy nor light. It was strange. I knew it was strange even then. I mean my world was about to turn upside down and inside out, and everything looked the same.

I opened the door slowly. My sister was talking to Ruth.

"Set a fork and knife by each plate," she was saying. "Cups too. Then you can go out. Johnny's in the tannery, but maybe you can help Jase or Owen in the barn."

Ruth was a methodical child. She picked up one fork and one knife and placed it next to a plate on the table. Then she went back for the next pair. Setting first the fork, then the knife. Then the cups. One at a time. Again and again. Twenty times. Then she brushed past me and out the door.

My sister slid four breads into the oven.

I picked up my bucket and emptied it into the tub.

"Need help?" I asked.

"Need help?" she repeated. "Need help? Why would you

think I need help? Of course, it's true last time I looked I didn't have four hands... But since you're my sister, you can work the churn for a while." And she began peeling potatoes.

It was quiet. A minute. Maybe two.

My sister tossed a potato into the stew pot. "I think there may be a slave in the barn," she said.

I stopped churning.

"A slave? A run-away slave? How do you know?" I asked.

My sister's eyes were black and narrow.

"Look at you," she began. "The same as always. Just one or two words and your hands are out the window. Can't you listen and do at the same time?"

I started to churn again.

"I'm listening and I'm thinking..."

"And being scared? Are you being scared?"

"Just thinking," I repeated. "And thinking doesn't have to be scared. Thinking can be sorry and worried... But, anyway, what did you see? How do you know?"

"Some food's been missing these last couple of nights," she said.

"That's hardly enough to tell. It could be rats, they come out on a milky moon, or squirrels, or maybe a coon."

My sister smiled.

"Rats? Squirrels? Coons? Next it will be a wolf or two."

"Stolen?" I asked.

She shook her head. "How could it be stolen? If someone is hiding someone, someone is going to feed that someone, at least until he leaves."

"Even if he is a slave?"

"Slaves eat like anyone else," she said.

It was quiet again.

Frederick was pulling a spoon against the wall, then trailing it across the floor. He circled the table. He came closer, jumping and bouncing, he and his spoon.

"Gidyap," he said.

"Should we go to the barn?" I began again.

My sister stirred the last potato into the pot. The warm smell of stew drifted into the room.

"Maybe more onions..." she was talking more to herself than to me.

"Just to see if someone is there..."

If she wasn't feeling into the onion bag, I'm sure she would have put her hands on her hips and turned her black eyes down on me. Well, down is the way it always felt she was looking at me, but she would really have to be looking up at me because I had overgrown her long ago.

"And what if we did go and sneak around and all that, what would we see? What do you think we would see? If someone is hiding, they're hiding. And even if we did see something, it would just be a man. No special wonderment in that."

"No, I suppose not," I agreed.

The stew was cooking. The bread was browning. The butter was creamy and smooth and thick.

"Besides, Mr. Brown would be angry," she continued. "It's his barn and his wanting to help and his food..." Her voice trailed off into itself. She didn't say, as she often did, and we're his hired help, just his hired help—until something else happens.

And I didn't say that anything else happened.

"Butter's churned," I said, standing up.

CHAPTER 4

MY SISTER LEFT. SHE HAD TO LEAVE. I didn't blame her. What else could she do? Could she fight with God? Could she fight with Mr. Brown? And what else could I do? I helped her pack. Not much. Enough to fill one bag.

"I didn't come with much and that's what I'm leaving with," she said, her voice trembling. "And that's what I'm leaving for—not much, just more and more of not much. You see, little sister," she said, trying to smile, "if you add not much to not much, it doesn't do anything, it doesn't change and it doesn't change anything. Not much is still not much."

The house we both came from. The house she was returning to. I could see it. Never big, never pretty, it was getting run-down. The porch rail was broken, window frames were cracked, stones were loose in the fireplace, neither bedroom had a floor.

A house and a barn right next to it, a corral that only had one horse, all just hunkered down in the woods, in the middle of trees and their tall, thick shadows—except for the garden. The only spot of sun.

"Well, that's what I know," my sister was saying. "And maybe that's not much." She shrugged. "There's that not much again," she said. "Can't get away from it. Always seems to creep in. Like dust through cracks. And you never know how many cracks there are till it comes time to clean. And the wind just blowing in cold. They say you never know how many cracks there are till the ship takes on water and sinks."

She stopped. She looked at a shawl I hadn't seen before—one of those shawls you wear for show, not for keeping warm. It was white, pure angel white, with strands of silver tinsel. She folded it carefully, slowly, and put it in her bag.

"But I don't think you'll be learning about that in school," she continued.

I watched the shawl disappear into the bag. I stood on one foot. Then the other foot. I bent down and looked under the bed to see if anything had been left.

"I don't know what I'll be learning in school," I said, crawling around the edge of the bed, feeling underneath it. "I don't think I'll need number learning because I know how to figure pretty well. It's just that Mr. Brown wants me to go, so I'll go."

"Is that what Mr. Brown said?"

I nodded.

"What did he do? Did he say plain out you're not quite smart enough? I could have told him that."

And then her voice softened.

"Going back to school... Imagine being a school girl at your age. Whoever would have thought it? Sweet sixteen and back in school."

"I'm almost seventeen, " I said. "And Mr. Brown says it's never too late to learn."

Her voice rose again.

"Mr. Brown. Mr. Brown," she teased. "Is that what you'll be calling your husband? You'll be calling him the same as a stranger?"

I didn't know what to say. Yes? No?

My shoulders tightened. I bumped my head on the side of the bed.

"Words were always hard for me," I said.

"Well, Mr. Brown is Mr. Brown and he must be right," she said more kindly. "And it's as true as every Sunday that you'll be learning words, a lot of words when you go to school."

I stood up.

"There's nothing left under the bed," I said.

She gave me that looking down look, but she also smiled.

"Silly Mary, anybody but a blind cow would know that, because everything's already here." And she closed her bag and turned toward the steps.

Of course, she had to go. And, of course, I wanted her to go so I could begin to find my new life, to make it real. But the other was also true. That I didn't want her to go. Or at least I didn't want her to go away like that. Returning to the house she had left, like a child returning from an errand. Like a child returning from an unsuccessful errand.

"Mama. Papa. I'm home."

Walking through town—where would she look? Would she return the stares? The whispers? Would she square her shoulders, lift her skirts and jump over the mud ruts in the road? Would she stop to look at that shell hairpin she always wanted to buy? Would she twist, even just a little, and look back through the forest?

"Mama. Papa. I'm home. It's me who's been sent home, not Mary."

My father would shake his head, turn his back, go out—say something about feeding the horse or mending the fence.

My mother would shake her head and cry. She would say the onions were making her cry. Then she would set my sister some chores. Stitch the frayed bed cover. Render the fat for soap. Clean out the fireplace.

And the days my sister thought she had left behind would begin again.

"Mama. Papa. I'm home."

"Mama, can I make a bread pudding tonight?"

"Papa, can I have a new pair of shoes?"

My sister. First born. The one who carried me piggy-back over the spring puddles and winter snow banks. The one who showed me how to milk, how to bellow up a fire. The one who braided my hair and fixed my weaving tangles. The one who taught me letters and how to write my name. The one who told me what to wear when it was the monthly time. And now, how could I forget? The one who had spoken to Mr. Brown. The one who said, "I have a sister." The one who opened the door, who opened his door, to my life. And what did Mr. Brown say to her?

"I like you enough, I trust you enough to hire your sister."

I saw her hesitate, then stop. Did she also want to go and not go? She turned to me. Almost a pretty woman. Almost delicate.

"How did you do it?" she asked. "How did you get him to ask?"

I shrugged.

"Spinning. I didn't do anything else," I said. "Just spinning."

The banging of spoons and pots. Johnny was trying his hand at baking bread. Jase was bringing in the milk. Owen was outside, leading the tannery horse around a mill that ground bark, with an eye on Ruth and Frederick.

"Smells good enough to eat," my sister said, turning from me, going downstairs, putting her hand on Johnny's shoulder. "But you also have to clean up—the butter, the flour, the eggshells. There's nothing finer than good bread but you know your father also likes a clean kitchen."

"Yes, ma'am," Johnny said, hardly looking at her.

She moved to the sideboard where Jase was pouring milk from pails to pitchers. "Slowly," she said to him, holding his arm, "but not too slowly."

"Yes, ma'am," Jase said, looking at me more than he looked at her.

She took a look around, turning on her heels.

"Well, it's time to go," she said almost to herself. And then more loudly, "At least it's time for me to go. Time for you to get on with your chores, little sister."

And suddenly, like a flash, I knew there was another reason I didn't want my sister to go. The house, the work, the children—it would be mine, I wanted it to be mine and I knew I could do whatever had to be done—but after she was gone I would be alone, all alone, with nothing and no one between me and Mr. Brown. Every day from morning till night. Every day and every night.

My sister didn't touch me. I wanted her to touch me, to touch my hand, but she didn't. And I didn't reach out to touch her. I just watched her open the door. There was a slice of sunlight and a warm breeze. Then she was gone.

I ran to the window. I saw her calling to Owen and Ruth

and Frederick. She picked Frederick up, felt his bottom to see if he was wet and kissed him. She hugged and kissed Ruth and put Ruth's lips into a smile. She shook hands with Owen then bent to kiss him on the top of his head. She patted the old horse on its gray mane.

And then the path. That path. The path we had come on. The path we had shared.

"Wait," I called leaving the window and opening the door. "Wait."

Wait for what I did not know.

"English," I called out "That's what Mr. Brown said I should learn. He said I should learn English and reading. He said that would make me smart."

I don't know if she heard me. She didn't turn around. She didn't stop walking.

I watched until she disappeared below the knoll by the tannery. Then I felt my heart. It was not light. It was not rippling like a pond. It was heavy, like stone. A stone. I felt as if I was about to tumble over an edge, down a mountain. The way stones do. But I was not a stone. I took a deep breath. I called Frederick in and changed his pants. I scrubbed the floor, set the table, seasoned the stew.

Then I rang the dinner bell.

CHAPTER 5

THINGS I NEVER THOUGHT COULD HAPPEN, happened. Dreams I never even dreamed, suddenly were real. Why? I didn't know. I never knew. But most questions are like that because most times your life just goes this way and that and you follow as best you can. And that's what I did. Besides, what difference would it have made? I did not choose. I had been chosen. I had been chosen to become Mrs. Brown, the wife of John Brown, the mistress of his house, the mother of his children.

At first, of course, people stared and whispered—never so you could exactly hear what they said. But once when I was in town with Johnny, I heard Mrs. Peters call me "that Day girl." And the other woman, hiding behind her parasol answered, "Hardly no bigger than her son."

Johnny was much like John. Into his own thoughts, into what he was thinking and reading. So I don't know if he heard them. But he didn't turn his head and he didn't say anything. He was leading the horse and wagon down the street and he just kept on going. Anyway, I was his Ma now. He knew that for sure, never making any trouble about it. And the other children never making any trouble either.

"Into the house," John had told them.

How clearly I remember that. His voice was so sturdy and straight. I remember that almost more clearly than when we said our vows, or when John slipped the ring onto my finger. No, I do remember the ring, John trying to slip it onto my finger. I remember because the ring was too small. I was twisting my finger as hard as I could and John was twisting the ring, but it wouldn't go on. I don't know how long we did that. Nobody saying anything. Nobody doing anything. Me, just standing there with my finger sticking out, pointing—at nothing. Then John put the ring back in his pocket.

"I don't need a ring," I whispered.

The minister cleared his throat. He put John's hand on mine.

"Before God and man, I now pronounce you man and wife," he said.

Words that flashed like lightning. And there was light. The light of a beginning. The light of seeing something around a corner. Beyond. Seeing something coming. My life coming. And I was going to meet it. No longer a girl, I was larger than I was and strong.

Of course, I knew my new life wasn't all mine. It was also Dianthe's. Not that I would exactly become her, but that my life would be built on hers. The life she had made. That I would join it. Standing, as she had stood, with this man in God's light.

"I now pronounce you man and wife."

Had she stood tall? Her back straight? Her eyes steady? Was she eager? Did she wonder? Was she afraid? A little...? Had she been as ready for her life as she was for her death? I turned my head, looked up, and I saw her—hovering there behind the children. Not a ghost, but how people said she looked. A slender woman with small hands and long thin fingers. And then for a second I saw, for a second I thought I could see her lying in her coffin and for a second I thought I could see John as he took the wedding ring from her finger.

The hush was over. The vision vanished. There was the scratching of a bench against the floor. The sound of feet shuffling. The seats in the tannery's little chapel had been filled and people were coming up to us. The men shook John's hand, the women nodded at me and smiled at the children.

"Into the house," John said when the neighbors, the journeymen, the well-wishers had gone.

We turned, walked down the stairs, past a row of vats, out the door, onto the path. It was July. Flies buzzed out from the barn. Bees were covering the clover. The sky was blue and endless until it reached the forest. That little yellow bird—it was singing.

We turned toward the house. We walked in single file, from the oldest child to the youngest, with Frederick holding John's hand. And then Ruth dropping back to hold his other hand. Quietly because it was the Sabbath.

The children expected nothing else. The Sabbath was a day of silence and prayer. It was a day of going into yourself to find more than yourself. It was a day to be sorry for your sins and to rejoice because God's goodness was in you. It was a day, as John said, to feel the power of the Lord.

A short walk and we approached the house, passing the tomatoes growing thick on the garden fence and the beans and onions beyond them. Then Johnny stopped, and so did Jase and Owen. They waited for John to reach them, to lead the way and open the door. Then, once again in single file, from the oldest to the youngest, we entered the house. The house that was different now.

Did everyone feel it? They must have, standing next to each other, the boys with their hands in their pockets, looking at the floor. The silence was not good now. It was heavy. It was cold. It was like a wall. I was no longer the hired help telling Johnny to chop more wood, Jase to bring potatoes from the shed, Owen to sweep the floor, Ruth to let the cat out and wash her hands and Frederick's too. I was their mother—but I didn't know what to say.

John motioned the children to gather around him. Looking at each child, he pointed to me and said, "This is your mother now."

Each child nodded. Even little Frederick. But no one said anything. No one looked at anyone. Then Ruth left John's side.

"Where are you going?" Jase asked.

Ruth didn't answer.

"Where she goes?" Frederick asked.

And when Ruth still didn't answer, he said, "Me too. Me too," and he toddled after her.

John raised an eyebrow but said nothing.

I said nothing.

Silence again until they returned, Ruth carrying a fistful of flowers. She walked past John and past her brothers. She came to me. She looked at me with her big, serious eyes and whispered, "This is for you. I picked these flowers for you, Mama."

Mama–the sound swelled up into the silence. It floated around us, all of us, I think, but especially from her to me. Mama–meaning that my life was in this house, with this man, with these children. That it would be my life. That it was my life. That there were things to do.

"Johnny, don't just stand there," I said. "Don't you know that flowers need water?"

"Yes, Mama," he said, taking the flowers to a cup on the sideboard.

John nodded and waited for him to return. Then he bowed his head. His voice was deep. It sang as much as it could on the Sabbath.

"We give thanks," he began, "to the Almighty who has seen fit to bring us to this time."

He raised his head. He looked at us.

We bowed our heads.

"Amen," we said.

"Let us pray," he continued.

It was 1833.

I was seventeen years old.

I knew about slaves who ran away to be free. I knew about Indians who came from the east and were being sent further west. I knew about people who didn't believe in God and who didn't go to church. I knew about all those things a little. But mostly I knew about what I had to do, what I had to take care of–the hand to mouth responsibility, as my mother said. And I knew what my hand to mouth responsibility was. It was Johnny, Jase, Owen, Ruth and Frederick, and keeping the house going with the food and the clothes.

Then it was night. And in the clearness that sometimes comes in the darkness, I knew what it was I had to learn. The big thing I had to learn—how to be Mrs. John Brown, at night, when the talking was over, when the journeymen were gone, when the prayers were over, when the children were in bed, when John had gone to his room—and when it was time for me to join him.

I wiped the table, hung the towel to dry. I swept the ashes from around the fireplace. I rearranged some weaving threads and wondered if I could get enough blackberries to use for dye. Wondering—and then suddenly remembering when I was little and sick with a boil festering on my neck. My mother had layered it with mud twice a day, then three times a day, but it got worse. So my father cleaned and sharpened his knife and I had to put my head on the edge of the woodblock like a chicken about to have its head cut off.

"Did you lie? Is that what happened? You lied, didn't you?" my sister asked, so excited she jumped from one foot to the other.

My mother was dipping an apple in honey to give me when the cutting was done.

"You better stand still," she told my sister, "before you get all gooed up with honey. Now that would be some mess, wouldn't it? Sticky fingers, sticky eyes and nose. You wouldn't like that none too much. Besides," she continued, "such foolishness. Boils don't always mean lying and sinning. Sometimes they just mean boils."

John was in bed. He was lying on his back with his arms folded under his head. He was watching the door but when I entered he turned his head from me. I think he closed his eyes.

I walked across the room. Did he open his eyes? Follow me? Would he watch me undress? I stretched my nightdress on the edge of the bed. I began—the apron, the skirt, the petticoat. I fumbled with the buttons on my blouse. I undid my breastcloth, let it slip from my body and pulled my nightdress over my head. More slowly now, I folded my clothes and put them on the chair.

John had turned the blanket back and his left arm was stretched across the bed. I lay down. His arm was under my back, around my back. His hand, his fingers circled around my side. His other arm came over me, slipping across my side to my breast. He held my breast. He held my breasts, one in each hand. He pulled a little, squeezed a little, then he put his hand between my legs.

"Take off your drawers," he said.

"Of course," I mumbled. "Of course, I forgot," my face burning red as I loosened the waistband, pulled it down and off to the side of the bed.

Then he was on top of me. Like I was a horse and he was the rider.

"Spread your legs," he said.

I spread my legs.

All I felt was his heaviness. His heaviness on top of me, pushing down on me. HIs heaviness pushing into me.

And then almost as suddenly as he started, he stopped and got off me. He sat up and straightened the blanket at the foot of the bed. Then he lay down and pulled the blanket up to his waist and over my chest and around my shoulders.

"Good night," he said.

"Good night," I answered.

And all I could think of was smoke. Butterflies disappearing in the thickness of smoke.

CHAPTER 6

TIME.

I never really thought about time that much. When I was a child I thought time would always be what it was. When it was winter I thought it would be winter forever and when it was summer I thought the days would always be long and warm. I never thought of time as being this year or that. I never counted on time, at least looking back I don't think I did. I never even thought to my next birthday.

Of course, when someone died you said how old they were. Like Dianthe died when she was thirty one years old and the first Frederick died when he was four. But those were their years. Not mine. That was time out in the sky somewhere, not in my life. Not sneaking into my life and haunting it. Shaping it—and then haunting it.

It was after I was married that time became more real—like a bucket of water or a loaf of bread. A new time that came and went. Coming mostly when John was asleep, his arms straight along his sides or tucked beneath his head. Or it would be there in the morning when my feet touched the cold floor and the rest of my body felt strong, but also shivered. And then in the spring. When I caught a glimpse of the yellow bird. When I saw a daisy popped up against stone.

It wasn't a waiting time. It was a knowing time—of exactly what I couldn't say. Maybe it was more of a feeling time. The feeling of time within me. The feeling of a child growing within me. The feeling that I was making a child and that the child I was making was making time... Did I dare to think forever?

Was I too willful? Too proud? Too sure?

I never said a word, but that didn't mean that God didn't know. It didn't mean that I wouldn't be punished. For a woman's sins. For the sin of thinking that my body was my own and that it could make life. For the sin of thinking, if only for a second, that my body could do anything, could become everything–like God.

Of course, it was a sin. It was blasphemy. It was worse than blasphemy because it was more than saying. It was a fist in God's eye, even though I never made a fist. My hands were strong. They carried, they opened, they held. They planted and cooked and wove and sewed and fixed. They gave. All those things but I never made a fist. Never.

And then time ended. Closed in on itself. Ending and starting. Coming together the way creeks do in the spring.

"I'm sure," I said. "It's my time."

"We will name the baby Sarah," John said.

CHAPTER 7

MY NAME WAS MARY BROWN. Her name was Prudence Crandall.

I lived first in Pennsylvania and then in Ohio. She lived in Connecticut.

"Mary Brown meet Prudence Crandall."

No, it did not happen. We did not meet. And if we did? "Will you join me for tea at the Seminary?" she might have asked.

Seminary? What was a Seminary? Would I have thought she said cemetery?

"We could talk."

Talk to a teacher? What could we talk about?

"We could talk about slavery. We could talk about freedom."

While I baked or cleaned or sewed? While I swept the barn, hoed the garden, fed the babies?

"It was summer when it happened."

Summer? Did she want to talk about the long days or the days that would follow them?

"The summer of 1833."

Yes, I remember the summer of 1833.

"I was arrested."

I was married.

It was a law. It said children of color couldn't go to Miss Crandall's school. It said Prudence Crandall should dismiss those children from her Canterbury Female Seminary, because white girls couldn't go to school with Negro girls, not even with one Negro girl, not even with one Negro girl who was almost white.

"You should know better," parents, neighbors, townspeople said. "If those nigger girls come here they'll never go back. They'll stay in town and become paupers."

"If you give those people a hand, they'll take a foot," they said. "Wouldn't think anything of it, just take all the jobs and drive the white folks from their homes. Is that what you want? Do you want your friends and neighbors driven into almhouses or else forced to the western wilds?"

"Haven't you heard the President?" they asked. "We have to show them who's boss. We have to move those black folks out same as we did the Indians."

"They're not white. They're not Americans. They don't belong here," they said. "We should send them back to Africa."

Prudence Crandall said, "No."

Prudence Crandall said, "I will teach whomever comes to my school, and if white girls won't come, colored girls will."

But I did not hear her. I did not see her. I did not know her. And I did not know Liza Harris, who was the first colored girl to come to her school.

"I would like to go to school," Liza said. "I want to be a teacher."

"Why do you want to be a teacher?" Prudence Crandall asked.

"Learning is like light," she said. "And to live in darkness is like dying."

The school was the most beautiful house on the village green in Canterbury, Connecticut. In the summer, looking from the windows of the second floor keeping room, you could see the neighboring fields of timothy, oats and barley. In the fall, after the harvest, cows might be in the stubby fields to take what the reapers had left. Pumpkins would be yellowing. The orchards would be red. All through town, porch posts would be hung with strings of quartered apples, sweet corn and peppers drying in the sun. And louder than the birds heading south was the creaking sound of the cider presses.

And then it was spring. From the keeping room windows you could see the curved backs of the farmers preparing their fields. Trees were coloring the sky a tender green. Robins returned to scratch the earth. Frogs and turtles were warming themselves on logs and stones. Crows watched from a distance. The heaviness of winter was gone. It was a time of beginning. A calling time—when it was right to open your door, when it was good to move into the sunlight.

Liza curtseyed. Her shadow was long and thin and graceful.

"Miss Crandall, ma'am, shall I tell the girls? Is it time for our walk?" she asked.

Prudence Crandall hesitated. "I don't know," she said. "There was so much trouble the last time we were out."

"But no one was hurt," Liza said quickly. "That stick came close but it missed me. And Mariah saw the chicken head coming and she ducked. And the stones were not much bigger than pebbles. Besides, we were hoping to buy some muslin and green cloth so we could make lilies. Amy's done it before. Cut and stitch and starch the muslin, and wrap the cloth around thin twigs. Soon it will be Easter and we wanted to put lilies in the kitchen and the keeping room." She smoothed her skirt. She looked toward the window. "Am I talking too much?" she asked.

"No, of course not," Prudence said. "It would be wonderful. Wonderful," she repeated. "And wouldn't it feel good to walk briskly and breathe deeply in fresh air?" She did not wait for an answer. She took Liza's hands in hers. "But what's brave and good can also be foolish. Even Reverend Kneeland would say there is a difference between forgiving and closing your eyes to danger. After all," she smiled, pressing Liza's hands more tightly, "we only have two cheeks."

"Yes, ma'am," Liza said.

"So we won't hurry. We'll wait. You know about fools and angels?"

"Yes, ma'am," Liza answered. "Fools rush in where angels fear to tread."

"Good," Prudence said, and then she added, "but you are

right. We should have lilies, and when my father comes the day after tomorrow, I will ask him to bring us a yard of muslin and long snips of green cloth."

Prudence tried to sound cheerful but beneath the lightness of her voice was the turning and tossing of all the nights she hadn't slept—when fear had come and anger. When she relived that walk. A simple walk that had become a scene of torment.

"Follow me," she had said. "Swing your arms. Exercise is good for the mind and body. And what's good for the mind and body is good for the soul."

Setting a good pace, around the square and past the pharmacy. Walking through shadows, in and out of the sun, a cool breeze, the scent of lilacs.

And then the surprise, the violence. And was there hate? Yes, there was hate, played as if it were a game. But it wasn't a game. Surely anyone would know it wasn't a game and she was certain that her bell would ring the next day. Or the next day. Or the next. She was certain that someone would come to say they were sorry. But no one came. Not the boys, not their parents, not her neighbors. They were not angry.

"Boys will be boys," they said.

"It's a prank," they said.

"There's no proof," they said.

The meanness, the wrongness, the hate and the hurt hung about the house like a fog. It was in their classrooms. It was in their bedrooms. It was in the keeping room where Prudence often wrote and sometimes waited.

And then, one day, it did happen. The door bell rang.

"I knew it would happen," Prudence whispered to herself. "Good is good and evil is evil and sooner or later it will sort itself out, and the good will shine bright and clear."

Prudence smiled. She was ready to listen, to understand, to forgive.

"Yes, they are boys."

"Yes, they made a mistake."

"Yes, we must teach them."

But when Prudence opened the door, it was the sheriff who was standing there and he was not smiling.

"I'll arrest your girls. I'll arrest every single one of them," he said.

"But we were only walking, exercising, singing a little..."

"The law is the law and the law says those coloreds can't come to this town. They don't belong here and they can't stay here."

"What can be wrong about learning?" Prudence asked.

The sheriff twirled his mustache. First one end, then the other. He did not come to talk about learning.

"I'll arrest them, and girls or no, I'll whip them ten stripes each on their naked bodies."

Violence again and hate. The hate of a man against young girls. The hate of white against black. Hate on the side of the law.

Prudence shuddered—suddenly remembering the first time she had seen a hog butchered. Heard it squeal. Saw it twist. Turn. Blood coming out of its nose.

"Will you stay for tea?" she asked.

"No," he said.

"No," she said, as if she had been asked a question, as if she had been given a choice. "I also say no, because God gives us no choice between right and wrong. No choice between light and darkness. No choice between love and hate. And this is a school..." she raised her voice just a little, to reach him as he was leaving.

Twenty girls. They came from Philadelphia, New York City, Providence, New Haven, Griswold, Canterbury. Twenty students. Thinking a door might open for them. Knocking on the door. Waiting. Willing to wait and work. They studied. They hoped. They prayed. They sang. Wearing white dresses, white bows in their hair, they sang:

'Tis here we come to learn to read
And write and cipher too;
But some in this enlightened land
Declare 'twill never do.

Studying. Hoping. Praying. Singing. But they were afraid of

the streets beyond the school. They were afraid of the man and the boys. And the nights were long.

"Don't be frightened," Prudence said when she saw the sheriff coming a second time. "I can see him from the window. I can see him," she said again, "and he is not carrying a whip."

And then the trial.

"Prudence Crandall, you did willfully and knowingly..."

"Yes," Prudence said. "Yes," she said softly. Again and again. "I am a teacher. And I believe in God."

The jury couldn't decide. The judge ordered another trial.

"Prudence Crandall, you did willfully and knowingly..."

"Yes," Prudence said again. "Yes. Yes. Yes. I am a teacher and I believe in God."

The judge charged the jury. His question, Are free blacks citizens? His answer, No, they are not. His question, Are free blacks who are not citizens entitled to the freedoms and protection guaranteed in the Constitution? His answer, No, they are not.

The jury was sure. Prudence Crandall was guilty, she broke the law, she was teaching black girls to be like white girls—to be like the best of white girls who were graceful and charming, who could understand the theories of St. Thomas Aquinas and recite the sonnets of Shakespeare.

Guilty.

Prudence was disappointed but hopeful. She was distressed but calm. She was not confused. She was not overwhelmed. She was gracious and gentle, even mild—but she would not give in. She went home to her school, her students, her life—to the comfort she saw in reason and learning and the love of God. She went home to letters of support and offers of help. She went home to letters of disapproval and warning. She went home to be a teacher and to await the outcome of her appeal.

It was a hot August morning when Theodosia went to fetch water from the well in the front yard and called out, "Miss Crandall, ma'am, come see what has happened."Prudence had just come back from Boston. She was at her desk, writing to William Lloyd Garrison. "I will be as harsh as truth, and as uncompromising as justice," he had written. "On this subject, I do not wish to think, or speak, or write, with moderation." And she answered, "If not for my faith in God I should fall like the fading leaf before the northern blasts. But we must be gentle with these people or their prejudices may burn even brighter."

"Miss Crandall, ma'am," Theodosia called again.

Prudence put her pen down. She sighed. She would have to remind Theodosia that ladies didn't bellow like bulls.

"Miss Crandall, ma'am," Theodosia said more urgently, lifting the bucket from the well as Prudence came out of the house and into the yard. Then she tipped the bucket so that Prudence could see into it. "What will we do? What will we do?"

Prudence did not understand.

"What will we do?" she asked. "I should imagine if you tip the bucket, you will spill the water. Isn't that so? And Isn't it almost time for poetry class?"

"Yes, ma'am," Theodosia answered, "but look..."

"Theodosia, child, you should know if the bucket is not full, it's because of the drought," Prudence began, glancing at the bucket, and then taking a second look, looking into the bucket. Looking, as if she was looking at a wall.

She hesitated for a moment. She took a deep breath.

"Go inside. It will be alright," Prudence said slowly and carefully as she took the bucket from Theodosia. "And don't worry. God is witness and judge. Always. Remember that. Always."

She hugged Theodosia, letting the girl's head rest on her shoulder.

"Yes, ma'am," Theodosia said.

Then Prudence turned away. Away from the bucket and the cow dung floating in it.

That afternoon Mr. Crandall came to visit. When he looked at the well, he shook his head.

"Prudence, I could see this coming. I warned you. Didn't I warn you? Didn't Hezekiah warn you? Didn't Reuben warn you? Anyone with two eyes, two ears and some sense between knew it was coming to this." He sighed, " and I don't know how it will end," he said, "but..." He hesitated only slightly. "If it comes to need I'll haul in water twice a week."

Of course, Mr. Crandall had never planned on traveling into town to bring his daughter supplies. He would just as soon wake up one morning to find that the town's preoccupation with colored school girls had disappeared like a bad dream. And he wasn't shy in telling that he would just as soon wake up one morning to find that his daughter's stubbornness had let go, had simmered down a little.

"Close the school. Move the school away from the center of town. Send the girls home so they can see their families and help with the harvest chores," he said, unloading bushels of dried peas and beans and a barrel of flour.

"No," Prudence said. "The girls like it here. They are learning here. They can read and write. They sing and sew. And Polly and Jeruska are even learning French. Mr. Burleigh teaches them and he says they are as quick as many white girls. Besides," she added, "their parents feel much for the education of their daughters."

"Prudence," her father clucked his tongue as he did when he was about to say something he would rather not say. "Prudence, look at me and listen to me. Your students are girls. They will go home, marry the boy on the next farm and have babies. Do they really have to learn French and give recitals on the pianoforte? Do they have to know the name of a stone not to trip on it? Do they have to know the pointing of stars in order to get home? Maybe they have learned enough."

Prudence said nothing. She just tossed her head and flashed her disapproving look—a little disbelief, a little shock and a large measure of disappointment. Mr. Crandall turned away. He pulled on his beard.

"It's just that I don't know how long the boycott will last," he said. "The people are angry."

"So am I," Prudence said. "But there's a difference," she added. "I am right."

CHAPTER 8

LIKE A MAN.

Not smiling and making do. Not cooking and turning away. Not confused and crying. I've seen that—a grown woman, crying like a child. Foolish like a child. Helpless like a child. Afraid.

Was that her sin? Is that why smoke filled the keeping room and flames crept between the clapboards? Is that why stones burst through bedroom windows? Is that why men stole into her yard, past the peach and pear and apple trees and beat the walls and door and windows with lead pipes and timbers? Is that why the sheriff did nothing, the neighbors said nothing? Is that why she shook her head, wrung her hands? Is that why she said, "It is too much. It is too hard."? Is that why she kissed each girl and said, "The school is closed. It is over."?

And wouldn't it be strange if her sin was being like a man and my sin was being a woman? If her sin was doing for others and my sin was doing for myself? If her sin was fighting for strangers and my sin was turning away and feeding my family?

"Mary Brown meet Prudence Crandall."

Could it have happened?

John came in.

"One less plate for dinner," he said. "I had to let one of the journeymen go."

"Again?" I asked. "One last week and one this week?"

He nodded.

"And next week? What will happen next week?"

Flies buzzed. I brushed them away from the milk jug and the pile of apple cores. They settled on Sarah. She started to cry.

"The baby is crying," John said, rocking the cradle.

He picked her up. He held her against his chest, his chin almost touching the black fuzz of her head. He walked with her back and forth, humming—I couldn't quite hear the tune.

Sarah stopped crying.

"Listening to hymns is only a step away from singing hymns," he said, patting her back.

Sarah smiled. Was it her first smile? Yes, I think it was.

Then Ruth came in, pink-cheeked and breathless.

"That cow chased me all around and then the one with big horns..."

In a second John stopped singing. He almost scowled. "Ruth," he said sternly, "were you in the corral?"

"The corral?" she repeated slowly. "The corral, papa?"

"Yes, the corral. Were you in the corral?"

"No, papa, it wasn't me. It was Owen who climbed the fence into the corral. And the cow, the new one, the one with big horns chased him..."

"Ruth," John said even more sternly, muscles about his mouth twitching a little. "Halt. Stop your tongue. Stop the lie before it burns into your soul. Can't you feel the fire?" He did not wait for an answer and it was true that Ruth didn't look able to give one. "Tut. Tut. Tut," he said. "You have let the Devil have his way with you."

He put Sarah in my arms.

"You know what we must do," he said to Ruth.

"Yes, papa," Ruth said.

He took Ruth's hand. They walked out the door to the barn.

Sarah was sleeping. I put her down in the cradle and went back to coring apples, setting them out by the fire to dry. Then I heard Jase and Owen. Neither one of them would walk if they could run. And Owen always bumping into things.

"Where's papa?" Jase called. "He's here. Uncle Frederick's here."

"Haven't I told you again and again don't be yelling so loud," I said. "And where's little Frederick?"

Sarah woke up and started to fuss.

Owen tripped on something and fell against the bushel of apples, sending apples every which way on the floor.

"I'm up here, mama. Way up here," little Frederick answered, sitting on his uncle's shoulders, his arms tight around his neck as they came in the door.

I wiped my hands on my apron. "A good day's welcome, Uncle Frederick. Please come in," I said, foolishly because he was already there, as plain as the door he had walked through.

Owen started to scoop up the apples. He tossed them into the bushel—the clunk of one apple hitting against another.

"Don't throw those apples like stones," I said more harshly than I meant to. "If they bruise you know they won't be good for drying."

Jase went to pick up Sarah. "Is she hungry?" he asked.

"Up here, way up here," little Frederick repeated.

"How do you like that, Mary... Two Fredericks together, one on top of the other. We're like an Injun pole I once saw," Uncle Frederick said, grinning so much you could see his teeth.

That's the way it was with Uncle Frederick. He was always saying something out of the way. And then you never knowing if what he said was just for the telling of it or if there was some meaning in it.

"I'll make tea," I said.

John walked into the house. Ruth was at his side. John said nothing. Ruth said nothing, but I could see the glisten of tears on her face. There was always that hard part of growing up, the whipping part.

"But she's not a horse," I heard my mother say once. Only once.

"But she's not a horse," I almost said.

"Bending the twig might hurt," John liked to say, "but the tree's all the better for it."

I filled the kettle, put it on the stove.

"Another plate for dinner," John said, taking little Frederick from his brother's shoulders.

Johnny came in. He handed his uncle two large saddle bags.

"Is the mare bedded down?" he asked.

"Yes, sir," Johnny answered. "I've put her in with two sheaves of fresh cut hay."

Uncle Frederick nodded but he hardly seemed to listen. He opened one of the saddle bags and took out two pork quarters. "It's been drained of blood," he said, "else on my way here I would have been tickled—or pickled—by a wolf or two. Those wolves are hungry. Seem to be more of them too."

John cleared his throat. He was not pleased. He stood up, his hands firm on the chair back.

"Frederick, I'm not about to be sowing seeds of falsehood," he began, "so it's no news that the vats are not as full as they were..."

He cleared his throat again—starting to speak, slowly, as if he were pulling up a long root without knowing the reason for it. Steady and strong, but watching out—for what I wasn't quite sure.

"And as long as the Almighty sees fit," he continued, "don't think, even for a minute don't think that we can't feed ourselves—and feed you, too."

John stared at his brother. John wasn't angry. Not really, Just hard. Looking hard. Sounding hard. It was man's talk and Uncle Frederick understood it. He said nothing, waiting for John to finish, flipping the straps of his shoulder bag up and down.

Then John lifted the chair back from the table and sat down. "But," he said, as he looked at each one of us, "I guess there's no earth-shattering reason to let good meat spoil, is there Mary?"

I took the meat to the sideboard. John was right. Most times we did have food. We had chicken, even beef when John couldn't sell one of the Thompson cows. But we didn't have pork in the longest time and a pork pie would be a mouth tempting treat. I sharpened the knife and measured the meat. There was enough for four pies, six if I went a little thin. And I had the flour, onions, and potatoes. I could have them steaming on the table for dinner if I hurried.

"Jase," I said, "put these apples away. I'll finish the coring tomorrow. Owen, bring in some eggs but look that you don't drop any. Ruth, you can get the cooking board and the bowls ready."

Jase put Sarah down and she began to cry. Little Frederick went to the cradle. He watched her cry for a moment, then he cried too.

I started the cutting because it had to be done. Besides, babies are always crying for one thing or another. They start and stop and most times you never know why. But Sarah wasn't frightful or given to fits. Sometimes she would let me begin the cooking or finish the cleaning before she howled. Sometimes when she was crying, if she didn't get too far into it, she would settle herself down a little. Look around. Maybe find her thumb and suck it.

But not now. Now her cry turned into a wail. A long wail. Her face turning red. Her feet kicking. Her hands closing into themselves.

"Sarah, my little Sarah," I said, picking her up, trying to hush her. "This is not a good time." But she did not hush and with my back to the table, I opened my blouse.

I did not have to turn her into me. I never did. Right from the time she was born, she knew how to find me. She knew how to grab and hold on. Tight. Sucking and pulling. Not letting go. Almost gulping. Milk spilling from the edges of her mouth.

So I cradled my baby with one hand, and with the other I was washing potatoes. Chopping onions. Crying a little.

John got the cups and was pouring tea.

"And what about Western Reserve College?" he was asking.

Uncle Frederick shook his head. "It's up and down there. Some days I think it's more down than up. More likely upside down. Who knows, maybe it's upside down everywhere..."

"That's slavery," John interrupted. "That's the sin of slavery. Turning the Bible around, inside out. Turning God's word against His children. Slavery is a mockery of Christianity. His will be done, Frederick. His will be done."

"That's for sure," Uncle Frederick agreed. "And that's what your friend, Elizur was saying. Reverend Beriah Green, too.

Clear as a church bell. No doubt they used more words in a month than most people use in a year. Going to meetings. Calling meetings. Anywhere they could. In church, out of church. Talking about slavery–man-stealing and man-selling–in their classes. Writing to the newspaper. Asking questions. 'If the Father is the same, aren't the sons brothers?' "

"Yes. Yes. Yes." John said, dropping sugar into Frederick's tea and handing it to him. "We know all that. But the answers. What were the answers?"

"That's a hard question. Maybe too hard. You know Elizur and Reverend Green left town."

"Run out? Were they run out like coyotes?"

"I wouldn't say they were run out exactly, but a lot of people were against them. There were meetings where they would start to talk but couldn't get to the end of what they were saying. Someone would start chanting, Send the blacks back to Africa. Then someone else would join in. Then another and another. Maybe there would be twenty people chanting, and then that's all that you could hear, Send the blacks back to Africa. Send the blacks back to Africa."

John pushed his cup away, spilling tea over the saucer, onto the table.

"But who are we?" he asked angrily. "How can we send them back? If they are free, can we send free men where they refuse to go? If they are slaves, can we send slaves if their masters refuse to free them? And if the slaves are freed, why should they be sent to Africa? Isn't this the land of freedom..."

Silence. An important silence. As if we were in church. How could anyone argue? How could anyone say no? "Listen," I almost said to the children. "Listen closely to what your father is saying."

But, of course, they were listening. They heard.

"People are afraid," Uncle Frederick was saying.

"People fearing people?" John asked. "People should be fearing Almighty God," he thundered, pounding the table.

"Afraid," he continued. "Every day and every night. In the streets. In the fields. In their homes. In their beds. Afraid to turn their backs. Afraid to close their eyes. They see black people with guns and knives. They see black people gone crazy, turned red with the blood of the white people they killed. They see Nat Turner in every black man. They see Nat Turner killing women and children. And they're afraid. Woefully afraid."

"But Nat Turner was not a free man," John protested. "And you cannot serve God if you are not free."

"I'm on your side. Of course, I agree. Absolutely," Uncle Frederick said. "But it's not easy," and he turned away from John, looking at the children, winking at little Frederick.

"Since when are we to be lulled by ease?" John asked. He stood up, his hands gripping the back of the chair again. "Since when do we let ease numb us? Since when do we let the promise of ease erase the promise of the Almighty? Since when do we let the charm of ease cover the face of God?"

"Well, you know what Elizur did?" Uncle Frederick asked, almost chuckling. "Come Commencement time he took himself a black man, a barber, and walked arm in arm with that black man, in the procession, just walking step by slow step down the aisle. Maybe there were a hundred white people in that auditorium and then that one black man. And Elizur had that black man sit next to him on the platform too. A hundred white people staring at one black man and no one said anything or did anything against it."

"But Elizur took the easy way out, didn't he? He left town. He ran away," John said impatiently. "And Reverend Green too."

"Can't argue about their being gone," Uncle Frederick said, "but if no one was listening, what choice did they have? They kept their lives and their voices and they're still fighting. And who knows, maybe the fight is just beginning. And don't foget about Mr. Garrison, running his paper every month. He'll never give up. No matter what, he's in this fight to the end. Telling the truth, with no easy words around it. He even wrote about Miss Crandall's school and how it had to close."

Suddenly John jumped up, his chair tumbling backwards.

""That's it, Frederick. Can't you see, that's the answer. The answer is schools," he said, hitting his hands together. "Negroes need schools for themselves and schools for their children. They need schools for their future and for our future, too. They need schools that won't close the way Miss Crandall's did."

Miss Crandall's school? Did I hear those words, that name, in my home, in my kitchen? Was I glad that she had a school? Was I sorry that she closed it? Was I surprised that she was a fighter? Did I know that she would lose, that she had to lose? Did I wonder why she wasn't a wife and mother? Is that why she lost?

And when it came to it, when it came to the very bottom of it, what was it that God wanted us to do? And how could we know? We could think, we could dream, but how could we know? Women... Maybe the knowing of women was different. But men knew. John knew.

And if I were a teacher, what would I have done? Opened my doors? Face the light and dark of whatever was there? The hate? How do you face hate? And my children? What would I have done with my children? Where would I hide them?

"There's not one school for Negroes anywhere," John was saying, "not even a Sunday school to shed light on the word of God."

Uncle Frederick nodded in agreement. Then he winked at little Frederick again. "If you get me some paper, I'll show you how we can get some of those pesky flies," he said.

"M-me," Owen said. "Sh-sh-show me."

"I'll show everyone, one and all, near and far," he said, "but especially those flies."

"Schools," John continued, his voice rising with excitement. "That's the answer. That's the only answer, Frederick. Without schooling, white or black, a man is less than a man. And a man who is less than a man is a slave—to himself as well as everyone else."

"What you're saying sounds like a miracle," Uncle Frederick said, rolling up a length of paper, "as if we could be guided through a tunnel by the light at the end of it. But it could be possible. After all, if a black barber can walk in an academic procession and sit on a college platform, anything is possible—even a miracle or two."

"We don't need miracles," John answered, his voice so strong it was shaking. "We need action. We need learning. We need schools. And we could do it. You know we could do it. You and me, we could start a school right here."

Sarah was in my arms, soft and safe. No one was chasing us. I could put her down. I could pick her up. I could put her to sleep. No one was coming out of the night, out of the dark places, with a gun or a knife. No one was going to drag us away, to pull us apart.

We were safe, in a place in the middle of other places, in the middle of other people. A place where you could turn your back. Lie down. Close your eyes. A place where you could put your hands away for a little while. A place where you could have a baby. A home, our home and a feeling between John and me—but then how could he start a school? Where would it be? Who would come? Where would they board? Who would feed them? And what if they were slaves and they were caught? And what if they were slaves and we were caught? And if they weren't safe, wouldn't we also be in danger?

Danger. Danger and hate, do they go together? And if someone was hiding in my house? And if they took John away? And if my children were screaming and if there was another man taking my children, another man on top of me, beating me...

Where would my life go? What would my life be?

I took a deep breath.

"I am Mrs. John Brown," I whispered to myself. "Mrs. John Brown. I was chosen. I was chosen."

"Now?" Uncle Frederick asked. "Should we open our school right now? Before dinner?"

"This is not a joking matter," John said angrily. "The time is always right to be righteous, or it is never right."

Safety. Feeling safe. Making a safe place. Having a safe place for Sarah as she turned her face from me, her fingers curling around my blouse, her eyes wide open—big and blue, her hair a fine dark color against pink cheeks, her forehead wrinkling and unwrinkling. Then her eyes closing into sleep. As if I had a magic hand. As if I could change something. Make something happen. But, of course, feeding a baby was not building a school. Feeding a baby was not freeing slaves. Feeding a baby was not hard or dangerous or frightful. It was not brave. It was not shining a light into that dark tunnel or crossing over on a rickety bridge. I don't know what it was. It seemed it was just one day after the next.

I shifted Sarah in my arms and buttoned my blouse. She wriggled, her mouth twitched and she turned to me again.

"No, my little Sarah," I whispered. "It's time to be through." And I smoothed the cradle sheet and put her down.

Then Jase came to rock her and keep the flies away. Owen came from the yard with four eggs. two in each hand.

"Look how many flies we got. Can you count them?" Uncle Frederick asked.

"I can count them," Ruth said, eager to show her learning, and she began, "one, two, three..."

Uncle Frederick sat down. He was serious again. "Open a school for blacks? It's possible, John. I suppose anything is possible..."

"And we won't turn tail and run from a God-given right," John said. "We won't tremble before our God-given duty."

I was chopping the pork, mixing the eggs and flour, turning in the onions, melting the butter. .

"It's our only hope," John said, pounding the table again. "Without schools, slaves will remain slaves. Masters will remain masters. And the wrath of God will descend on us all. I tell you, we can't let that happen, Frederick. It's a sin. It's a black mark on our souls."

They reached the end of their talking. It was quiet. I could hear a wolf in the distance. Nearer by, that sad bird—John said it was a whippoorwill.

I sprinkled the pies with pepper and put them in the oven.

Jase put more wood on the fire. Then he came to stand squarely between John and Uncle Frederick. "Look at me and see that I am grown," he said. "I can haul water. I can split wood. I can plow a field. I can build a house. And I can build a school."

"So you can," John said, his face coming slowly into a smile.

Owen lifted his bad arm, held it as high as his shoulder, then let it swing it back and forth.

"B-but s-snakes are b-better than s-schools," he said. "Do you want to see a r-rattlesnake?"

John gave Owen one of his powerful looks. "Talking comes from thinking and if you talk foolish, you will think foolish and if you think foolish, you will be foolish, but for sure there will be no foolishness in this house..." he began.

Uncle Frederick turned around to look at Owen. "It's alright. You can tell me about your rattlesnake, big fella," he said. "Do you have a rattler in your hat? Is that where it is?"

"N-no," Owen said, trying to talk slowly so he wouldn't stumble over his words. "You're just making f-fun, Uncle Frederick. You can s-see I don't even have a h-hat."

"Is that so? No hat for my nephew? Well, we'll just have to get you one. Maybe a hat with a big brim like a cowboy? Or a high black hat..."

"Enough," John interrupted. "We're talking about opening a school for blacks and keeping it open. We're talking about reading and writing, learning the gospel, living the words of God." Then he shook a finger at Owen. "And if you fool with a rattler, I may be burying the rattler and you together."

"Anyway, it's probably some old black snake," Jase said. "There's lots of those black snakes in the field. They're sorely big but they'll slink away faster than you can run after them."

"It's not a b-black snake. It's a r-rattlesnake," Owen insisted. "I saw the r-rattles," and he held his fingers four or five inches apart.

No one said anything.

"And I h-heard the r-rattles too," he continued, looking sideways at John.

Little Frederick started jumping up and down. He waved his hands in front of him. "Me. Me. I want to see," he said.

Ruth looked from Jase to Owen to Frederick and back to Owen. She looked at him for a long time, as if he held the key to a special secret. "Me too," she said. "I'm not afraid. I want to see too."

"Stop it," John said, his voice rising. "This foolishness is running away with itself just when we need to be serious and steady and look slavery in the eye and talk about a plan. Jase go get Johnny. Owen sit down. Ruth, you won't understand much, but you can listen too. Frederick, you take care of Sarah. And remember not a word of this to anyone."

"Why not?" Jase asked.

"Because we're not ready yet," John said.

That night when I put Ruth to bed, I saw the thin whip mark on her back.

"Does it hurt?" I asked.

"Papa loves me," she said. "And God loves me too."

CHAPTER 9

THE NIGHT BEFORE WE MOVED I dreamed about the black barber. His name was Elijah. He was cutting my hair. But wherever he cut, my hair would curl up tightly, the way it is with black people. I wanted to tell him to stop. Couldn't he see that I was white?

I was afraid. I was afraid he would cut me. I was afraid he would make me black. I was afraid he would make me black and someone else would cut me. I ran and ran. And then I did a terrible thing. I sent Johnny, Jase, Owen—even little Frederick, to the barber. Only Ruth I kept at my side and Sarah in my arms.

It was almost summer. When I thought about it, I told myself that summer would be summer anywhere. Do you think the sun rises only in New Richmond, Pennsylvania? I would ask myself. Or, Do you think there is no fresh breeze, no green trees, no good earth and clear water, no little yellow bird in Franklin Mills, Ohio?

John loaded the wagon. The plough, the axe, the hoe. The pots, the crockery, the big tub for washing. One spinning wheel, the small one, and the loom. Our bed—taken apart, looking more like fence posts or firewood. Books. John's books. Johnny's books. And the Bibles. Eleven Bibles.

Of course, I never expected there would be a send-off party and there was none. And no one said remember this or remember that. No one said remember the good days. No one said remember the long winter nights by the fire. The children did go—I think all of them went, one by one except Sarah, following Johnny, to the graves. Jase pulling weeds from Dianthe's grave. Ruth bringing an armful of flowers. Frederick following her—more whimpering than crying, stopping to look at the baby's grave.

It was my first leaving and I did not look back. Now I wonder about the house, what happened to it. Did someone find it, move in? Run-away slaves? Indians? Was it taken down and sold for shingles? Would someone from the town or the forest notice that the smoke was gone?

John looked around. Not at the house, but into the distance. He shielded his eyes and looked at the sun.

"We'd better hitch up and get started," he said. "That halo means rain before the day is out."

So we started. The oxen pulled. The wheels squeaked and turned. The wagon bumped and jostled. We were at the creek, over the bridge. We were crossing the meadow, at the edge of the forest.

Forward. We were going forward. As much to find our lives as to make them. "The Kingdom of Tomorrow," John sometimes said.

I heard a wolf. I thought I saw Dianthe—was she waving us on or waving us to come back? And the Indians, shadows themselves, slipping in and out of the forest shadows.

Johnny, Jase and Owen rode the horses. Ruth and Frederick were in the wagon. Sarah squirmed in my lap and I let her go to join them.

The sun coming up over the trees, through the trees. The warming felt good.

"And the water came from the Great Lakes and covered the land," Johnny was saying.

"Was that in the Bible?" Jase asked.

"No, that was in Ohio," Johnny answered, almost as if we were all sitting by the fire and he was reading to us from his book.

"Was it a f-flood?" Owen asked.

Johnny nodded. "Yes, that's what it was. It was a flood."

"Wrong, wrong, wrong," John called out to them. "Johnny is sure as Satan wrong. It wasn't a flood. How could it be a flood? There was only one flood..."

But Owen's horse had stumbled and started off and Johnny and Jase were after catching up to him.

I took out my mending. The coarse work I could do between the shoves to and fro—the ruts, the ditches, the stones, the slopes up and down.

Then we came to a marshy place. Grasshoppers, springing up from nowhere were everywhere. Crunching under the wagon wheels. Hitting against the sides of the wagon. Whirring past our faces. One landed in my hair.

"Mama, there's a hopper in your hair," Ruth said, crawling out from the back of the wagon, to the edge of the seat, to see if she could catch it—but the wagon suddenly jerked to a side and Ruth tumbled out and down into the mud.

"Whoa, ye. Whoa," John called and stopped the oxen.

The boys came back. Jase swung down from his saddle to help Ruth climb back into the wagon. But John shook his head. "Walk alongside for a while," he said to her. "Give you time to think about being wild and foolish. Give you time to thank the Lord he didn't break your legs or your back. And it wouldn't hurt none too much for some of that mud to cake up and dry off."

I reached into my mending pail and gave Ruth a cloth to wipe her hands and face.

Frederick began to cry.

Sarah was hungry.

"Use the cloth on your face first," I told Ruth, "before it gets too dirty from the mud on your hands."

"I think it would be proper to say it was a flood," Johnny was saying.

"God's covenant," John's voice boomed in answer. "You have forgotten God's covenant. Or do you think that God Almighty has forgotten His own covenant? Didn't He say, No more floods? Have you forgotten the rainbow?"

Ruth handed the cloth up to me and I hung it over the wagon's edge. It would be dinner time soon—fish cakes, corn meal bread and dried apples. Then I could find a creek and wash the muddy clothes. Maybe there would be a small spring waterfall where I could wash Ruth's hair.

The flood. I could see a wall of water. A house of water with nothing in it—not even frogs or fish. A wash of water. A big tub of water running away with itself. The earth bulging, pressing in on itself, swelling. The earth getting big with water.

And a rainbow. Did I see a rainbow once? Yes, not then, but later. From the sky to the meadow to the graveyard as we were leaving. Just beyond the graves. Almost like a road.

And behind my thinking I could hear Jase ask, "But what about the people? If there was a flood, what happened to the people?"

And I could hear Owen say that we needed guns. More guns. "Papa, we need g-guns for the forest, for the wolves and the bears and the panthers... "

CHAPTER 10

WE ALWAYS HAD A GARDEN. Whenever we moved. Wherever we were. When we were in Richmond, Pennsylvania. When we moved to Franklin, Ohio. When we moved north to Hudson, Ohio.

"It will be better here," John said.

"It will be better there," he said.

"It will be better here," he said.

"It will be better there," he said.

And again back to Franklin and again to Hudson. Then to Richfield. Yes, even in Richfield, in that place of terror and pain, in that place of trial and darkness and death, even there I had a garden. I remember corn, tomatoes, peas, beans, turnips, potatoes, onions and pumpkins—so big and round and orange.

From place to place. From house to house. In front of the house. In back of the house. To the side of the house. Wherever there was a little sun. It was the first thing I did, before I unpacked or sorted clothes or hung a clothesline or the curtains. And many times in the spring and summer when the moon was full, I'd stay up all night working the garden, trying for a few more rows, hoping for a few more plants.

Those nights Ruth was in charge of the babies and when one woke up she would tend to it and it if got too loud or red-faced and she couldn't satisfy it, she would bring it to me. First Sarah. Then Watson. Then Salmon. And then the other babies, Charles and Oliver. And after Oliver was born, Sarah was old enough to do the tending and sometimes Watson helped. And then there were the new babies, Peter and Austin.

Of course, the babies weren't the only worry. There were

animals—raccoons and skunks. Deer would come. And bears. The big animals would push the fence to get in. The little animals would squeeze through the fence or burrow under it. And then there were the birds. The black birds that turned the sky black when they came—hissing more than chirping. And the worms, the mites, the beetles, the ants, the caterpillars—there was no way to keep them out.

And then there was the time the rats came. It happened only once but I think it was the worst. Johnny was just home from studying at the Grand River Institute and he heard them first.

"Stop singing and listen," he said, interrupting Sarah who was singing one of John's favorite psalms,

'We have heard with our ears, O God,
our fathers have told us,
the deeds You did in their days,
in days of old...'

"Listen to the gnawing. It's rats or woodchucks," he said, running out of the house, waving his arms like a wild man.

Even before I got the hoe, Jase was out the door with his poking pole and Owen was right behind him with the axe. Ruth grabbed two pans and was banging them as hard as she could to scare away whatever pestilence was out there. And Frederick was taking off his shoes and running past Ruth to catch up with Jase and Owen.

So there we were, packed into the garden which really wasn't more than a patch at that time and maybe at the end we ruined more plants than the rats did. And Owen with his bad arm was hollering and swinging the axe. And what with Frederick throwing his shoes at shadows and rushing headlong after them, I could see him cutting his foot on the axe before he would know what was happening.

"I'm working, Mama," Frederick said when he saw me looking at him. "Tell Papa that I'm working."

"Yes, when Papa comes home, I will tell him," I said.

"Jase, you can tell Papa that I'm working, can't you?"

"Sure," Jase answered.

"Sure," Owen agreed.

"And we'll get those rats. We'll get all of them. We can get a million rats if we want to, can't we Jase?" he asked.

"Sure," Jase answered.

"Sure," Owen agreed.

"Because we're strong and we're fast and we're working," Frederick said, throwing his shoes again.

"Sure," Jase answered.

"Sure, Owen agreed.

Trying to catch rats, to corner them. As soon as I lifted my hoe to one, it was over to the next stalk or stem or flower, tearing it down, chewing it up—with a sound almost as if it was laughing.

A laugh is worse than a howl, more like a demon, more like the devil's work. That's what John would say—I could hear him saying it as I was twisting this way and that, striking rats, watching them break or bleed or bare their teeth—finally to turn tail and disappear.

I stood up.

"It's over. They're gone," I said, feeling pains slowly creep into my arms and back. Pains in my stomach too. A dull pain. Like something was pushing or pulling or tearing. I worried about that—about the baby I was carrying in me, but there was nothing to be done for it.

I turned to the house. "We'll have to wait till morning to see what we can save," I said. "And Frederick, don't forget to pick up your shoes."

A short walk to the front door. It squeaked as I opened it.

"It's over. It was rats and they're gone," I said to the little ones.

But as soon as my eyes got used to the darkness, I saw that it was not over. There was Sarah, my little Sarah not even five years old, holding Salmon in her arms, with Watson at her side. There she stood, in front of a sack of flour, facing down a rat.

"You better not," she was saying. "God is watching. He sees you. He sees you. He sees you," she repeated.

"Don't move," I said to Sarah, inching toward her and slowly lifting my hoe, swinging it swiftly at the rat, chopping as if my hoe was a hatchet. The strike was true and it caught the rat in the middle of its back. Its mouth opened, its legs curled and its body slumped onto its side.

"Is it dead, Mama?" Sarah asked.

"Yes, it's dead," I answered.

"Do we have to bury it?" she asked.

"Berries?" Watson asked, moving from behind Sarah. "Does Sarah have berries?"

"The middle of the night is no time to be thinking about berries," I said.

He started to cry.

"But Sarah has berries and I'm hungry," he said.

"Watson, do you have frogs in your ears? Can't you hear what I'm saying? Sarah doesn't have berries. Ruth doesn't have berries. No one has berries."

"All gone?" Salmon asked, wriggling from Sarah's arms to stand next to Watson. "Berries all gone?"

"All gone? Yes. All gone," I said, picking him up and taking Watson by the hand. "The rats are all gone and it's time for bed."

"But the rat, Mama," Sarah called after me. "Do we have to bury it?"

"It's a varmint," Johnny said as he came into the house. "And you don't bury varmints. You just get rid of them."

Watson started to cry again. "Berries," he said. "I want berries."

The others came in.

Frederick gave Watson one of his shoes to play with. "Don't cry, Watson," he said. "Nobody eats in the middle of the night, do they Jase?"

"Nobody," Jase said.

"Nobody," Owen agreed.

"See, " Frederick said, "And I would tell Watson and Salmon if someone was eating, wouldn't I Jase?"

"Yes, you would," Jase said.

Owen, who had come close to the rat, almost stepping on it, raised his axe, looked at it, and said nothing.

I lit one candle and gave it to Johnny. I lit a second candle and gave it to Jase. I lit a third candle for the rest of us.

"We need a little light to settle down before we go to bed," I said.

The candles flickered, each making a small circle of light.

Ruth went to stand by Johnny. Jase, Owen and Frederick stood together. Sarah was close to me.

"Mama, it's still there," she said. "Its eyes are open and it's looking at me."

"But we're all standing here together, so how can it be looking at you?" I asked. "Besides, it's dead, so It's not looking at you. It's not looking at anyone. And anyway, you weren't the one who killed it."

It was quiet. It seemed as if we were all around that rat waiting for something to happen. But maybe it only seemed that way. Maybe we weren't even looking at the rat. Maybe what we were looking at was its death. Did Sarah see that too?

"Its eyes are open, so how can we bury it?" she asked.

Johnny gave his candle to Ruth. Then he got the fireplace shovel, slid it under the rat and took it outside.

Frederick left Jase and Owen. He came over to Sarah. "Want to play with my shoe?" he asked.

Perhaps she didn't quite hear him. "I want to see if the rat is dead," she said. "Mama," she asked, "how long can a rat stay dead?"

"D-dead is dead," Owen said, "b-because rats aren't people."

"But its eyes are open, so how can we bury it?" Sarah asked again.

Frederick put his hands over his ears. He looked down, at the floor where the rat was. At a spot of blood.

"God will do it," he said. "I know it."

"Do what?" I asked, but Frederick didn't answer, just went back to putting his hand over his ears. And then he started to cry.

"God is good. You know that," I said, drawing him to me, putting my hand under his chin, trying to make him look at me. Trying to make him smile. Wishing that John was here, that he could tell them, explain to them. That he could read to them from the Bible about killing and death. "And God does watch," I added. "And God does His way and His will."

The candles were burning low.

"We'll have to make more," Ruth said.

Watson and Salmon were waking, calling out.

"Mama. Mama. Papa. Papa."

"Papa is not here. You know that," I said, covering them. "But we are here, all here together. And we saved the garden and we killed the rats and we'll have a good breakfast in the morning."

The pain in my stomach. The pain in my back. My eyes closing. It would be good to go to sleep. To get ready to fix what needed to be fixed, to cook what needed to be cooked, to sew what needed to be sewn, to weave what needed to be woven, to make what needed to be made. And the roof—I had forgotten, it was leaking again.

"Yes, soon," I said, "we'll have to get to the candles before the days start getting too short."

Johnny came in. He put shovel back by the fireplace.

"There's a new light some people have. A kerosene light," he said. "It uses coal oil and..."

"But it costs more than we have," Jase said.

"I don't care. We have other things," Ruth said, blowing out her candle, turning to bed. "Anyone can have a light."

CHAPTER 11

WINTER CAME EARLY THAT YEAR. Only November and the fields were white with snow and the wind twisting around itself, around every tree and stump. Sometimes whistling behind the barn, up to the front of the house. Piling up snow. Piles as big as carriages that were going nowhere. Piles as small as graves. And still snowing. Turning into a storm. John was home that night and when it was time he took the sleigh to fetch the mid-wife. The bells of the sleigh disappearing into the wind.

We were still living in Hudson, in that nice white farmhouse—maybe that's why I wasn't worried about how we would make do. It wasn't that John kept secrets—he never did, and he was not shy in telling me that things were bad. One plan after the other fell by the wayside. We were losing the land by the canal. We were losing the land by the stagecoach road. We were losing the land we bought for a mill site and the land we bought for the water company. We were losing the land we were going to sell when the town got bigger. I saw the bills. I heard the talk.

"Mr. Oviatt wants his money back."

"Mr. Wadsworth wants his money back."

"Mr. Kent wants his money back."

Maybe it was that I couldn't see that far into the future, the way some people do. Maybe it was that I trusted John so much, maybe too much. And that house—maybe it was too comfortable. I remember the fireplace, ten feet long I think it was—studded with hooks for pots and pans and ladles, even a small shelf for a kettle.

And John was always saying, "Narrow thinking will turn on

you like a starving dog." So I was trying not to think too narrow. I was trying to look to the side of me, up and down. Away from me. To look across the field. Across the road. To see beyond myself and my family. And seeing beyond that was to see the black man. The black woman. The black child.

"Will you do it?" John asked.

We were seated around the fireplace.

What did he say? That he wanted to make war on slavery? That it was his duty? Yes, he said slavery was a festering wound, a poison for the body and soul and it was his duty to destroy it.

Did I ask, how will you destroy it?

Did I ask, who will help you?

"I will devote my life to break the jaws of the wicked and pluck the spoils out of his teeth," he said.

Did I ask, what about me? What about the children? Who will help us?

Did I remember our marriage vows, "forsaking all others until death do you part...?"

Did I see my sister, standing over me, laughing at me? Look at you, she was saying, you're scared.

Then John folded his hands in front of him, almost as if he was praying. And he began to tell a story about a man, a young black man, whose name was Amos. He was a husband and a father and a slave. And every day except Sunday, he went to work in the fields. And every day at dusk he came home. But one day when Amos came home from the fields, he found his cabin door open and when he went inside he saw broken dishes and scattered clothes but he didn't see his wife or little girl. The cabin was small, only one room and there was no place to go, no place to hide, still Amos looked for his wife and child. Behind the bed. Under the table. In the corner shadows. Fearing the worst, he went running from the cabin, looking, calling Jennie... Jennie... Running, when the foreman Big Joe stopped him.

"Turn around and go on home," he said. "There's nothing to be done. She's been taken down the road."

Amos did not listen to his ears. He listened to his heart. He thought he heard Jennie crying Amos... Amos... He thought he heard his little girl crying daddy... daddy... "I'm coming," he cried out. "Amos is coming. Daddy is coming."

And he began to run away from the master's house, the wide porch, the green lawn, away from Big Joe standing there, his hand on his whip.

Amos ran on down the road into the dark, calling on God, calling on the Lord Jesus for help. He ran as fast as he could, his heart beating in his ears—but even so after a short while he heard the earth pounding and he knew that there were horses behind him. Coming closer. Then one, two, three, four arms were on him, around his neck, pinning his arms to his back, throwing him down, tying him up. And he said nothing to them, nothing to those arms, those faces, only calling out for his wife and child.

"I'm coming for you," he said. "Look behind your shoulder, I'm coming for you."

But the men who held Amos laughed at him and kicked him. Then they covered him with hot tar and turkey feathers and dragged him back up the road to a big oak tree. And all the while Amos was crying out, moaning, "I'm coming. I'm coming."

And when the men got to the tree, they tied Amos to it and began to whip him. All of those men took their turn whipping him. And they whipped him until you could hardly tell what it was they had against that tree that they were whipping..."

John's voice ended. Then he almost whispered, "Remember them that are in bonds as bound with them," he said. "Remember…"

And suddenly I could see that woman, that Jennie, and my hands were torn and bleeding. My face was bleeding. And my heart—it jumped from my chest and I was following it down the road. And I was holding my baby, my Sarah. And the men were coming. The white men and the horses.

And God? Where was God? And John? Where was John?

The fire was burning low. Jase carried two logs to it and stirred up some embers. We were all watching—John, Johnny, Jase, Owen and myself—as the flames began to leap up and into each other, into more light and warmth. The only sound was Frederick whimpering in his sleep. And then the fire hissing with wood that was not quite dry.

John turned to me first. Half of his face lit by the fire. The other half in darkness.

"Mary, will you do it?" he asked. "Will you make common cause with me? Will you promise to help me blast this darkest evil to the hottest pit in deepest Hell where it belongs?"

Did I say I was afraid? How could I say that? I remembered Stubbles—he had been afraid. I remembered Clemson—he had been afraid. I remembered Zachariah—he had been afraid. And that woman—the one who was afraid to tell her name, even to John. Hugging her children. Stuffing rags in their mouths when they needed to be quiet. Hiding her children, behind a haystack, in the hollow of a tree, the little one under her skirts. Running away. Hoping to get to Canada. Needing to get to Canada where they could raise themselves up, where they could cry out to the Lord and be heard.

But I was a free woman, and that meant I was free to do my duty and free to do what needed to be done.

Remember them that are in bonds as bound with them.

Yes, I was a free woman. I was free to listen to words, the words of God, the words of my husband.

"Yes," I said. "I promise."

Then John turned to each of the boys.

"Johnny, will you make common cause with me against man's most vile sin?"

"Yes, sir," Johnny said. "I promise to be with you."

"Jase, will you too make common cause with me until this evil is nothing but a hateful memory?"

"Yes, sir," Jase said. "I am eager to make common cause with you and stand beside you in this fight."

"And, Owen, what will you say? Is slavery so ugly that it will speed you into action?"

"Yes, sir," Owen said. "I am ready for the fight."

"Let us pray," John said as he got down on his knees.

We joined him on our knees. Our heads bowed. Our hands folded.

"Except the Lord build the house, they labor in vain that build it; except the Lord keepeth the city, the watchman walketh in vain."

"Amen," we said.

Then John stood up and raised his right hand and we did the same.

"Repeat after me," he said.

"I do solemnly swear," he said.

"I do solemnly swear," we said.

"To keep the promise we have made in its entirety"

"To keep the promise we have made in its entirety"

"To hold the sacred secret in our hearts no matter how difficult or dangerous"

"To hold the sacred secret in our hearts no matter how difficult or dangerous"

"To nourish it and carry it wherever we go"

"To nourish it and carry it wherever we go"

"Until the end."

"Until the end."

Did I ask, when will we start—today or tomorrow?

Did I ask, how long will it take? One year? Two years?

Did I wonder about my heart—was it big enough, strong enough...

The moment was over.

Frederick was still whimpering. Salmon started to cough. Then Watson. Following after Sarah in the cough that she had, but she was easier taking her medicine than the babies were. Only once, the first time, did she blow the pepper off the spoon. The other times she just squeezed her eyes shut and said "I pray the Lord my soul to keep" and swallowed.

John banked the fire. The boys carried the chairs back to the table.

"Good night," John said, shaking hands with each of them. "Let us hope and pray that the Lord looks favorably upon us..."

The boys—even Owen, looked older in the gray light. They

nodded. "Goodnight, sir," they said, turning, walking slowly down the hall to their room.

I started after John, then stopped. Taking two candles from the shelf, I lit them and found the pot I wanted and the vegetables I would boil down to make a sweet syrup, something that the pepper would stick to, something sweet enough for the babies to swallow. And if the coughing got worse, they would need a plaster—but that would be hard, keeping the hot cloth strapped to their chest, ten minutes at a time.

Still November.

A rooster crowed.

Charles was born on that snowy day in 1837.

And the next day at Union College, Professor Hickok rode through town, calling at every house.

"Come to a meeting at the Congregational Church," he said.

And when John came home from that meeting, his face was almost as white as the snow and his eyes looked like steel.

"He's dead," John said. "Murdered."

CHAPTER 12

HER NAME WAS CELIA ANN FRENCH.

She had blue eyes and she was beautiful.

"She is pious, intelligent, refined, and of agreeable manners. She is also sweet-tempered, obliging, kind-hearted, industrious, good-humored, and possessed alike of a sound judgment and correct taste. And," he added in a letter to his mother, "she loves me."

"Are you willing to leave your home and come to a place where people may outright shun you?" he asked her.

She answered without any hesitation. "Yes, I will do that."

So Celia Ann French and Elijah P. Lovejoy were married on March 4, 1835 in her parents' house in St. Charles, Missouri. They ate well, were showered with rice and good wishes and returned to St. Louis to live together as man and wife, to live dutifully and faithfully to each other and God.

Lovingly.

But Elijah was right. There was anger. And Celia had never known that kind of anger, that kind of meanness.

"My husband is a man of God," she wrote to her mother. "He preaches God's word. He believes in God's love and mercy and forgiveness. But there is so much misinformation, so much mistrust, that anger seems to settle down heavily upon us. Sometimes I think it might crush us. But then I remember our love, so fine and uplifting, that I cannot be sad or afraid for too long."

So Celia smiled at her neighbors. Chatted with them when she could. Cooked for Minerva when she was sick with the flu. Sewed a christening dress for Gretchen's baby. And sometimes read or wrote letters for old Leatty, who had raised three families—her mother's, hers and her daughter's—but had never gone to school.

Smiling, even happy in spite of the anger.

"It's like the sea," she said to Elijah one evening after they had received a threatening note.

Elijah raised his eyebrows. "Like the sea?" he asked.

She took his hands in hers, raised them to her cheek. "What I mean is the anger is like a wave or two upon the sea. But beyond the waves the water sparkles, all the way to the edge of the horizon. Shining and sparkling."

She kissed his hands. He kissed her hands.

"You are my strength," he said. "My joy and my strength."

But people were angry, very angry. And waves crash.

"Why don't you let a certain subject alone?" they asked her husband.

"Slaves have souls," Elijah said.

"You will be driven from the streets, from the church, from the city," they said.

"I will not be driven from my calling or my conscience," he said.

"A newspaperman is not God," they said.

"How much more that holds true for a slaveholder," he said.

Preaching from his pulpit. Teaching in Sunday School. Writing in his newspaper.

Coming home in the evening. Turning to his wife. Taking her in his arms. Stroking her hair.

"They broke into the office today," he said. "They say they are righteous men but they are hooligans, all of them. Smashing the press, dumping it in the river..."

"I know," she said quietly.

"But I cannot give up the rights of conscience," he said. "And what is freedom of opinion if there is no free press?"

"I understand," she said.

"I cannot connive at what I believe to be sin for the sake of popularity," he said.

"I understand," she agreed.

"We may have to move," he continued more slowly, not looking at her.

"Moving is not the same as being driven," she said, putting his hand gently to her stomach. "Feel our son. He is strong like his father."

Elijah felt the baby kick. Then he lay back and breathed deeply. "Yes, and strong like his mother," he said. "Truly we have been blessed."

But anger. So much anger. The only place it could go was into hating. And the anger and the hate followed them from the slave state of Missouri to the free state of Illinois.

"You must act with caution," his friends said.

"You must watch out for the mob," they said.

"Be watchful as you come home from church tonight," they said.

The night. A clear night. So many stars shining. Their room was almost bright with starlight.

And then the banging on the front door.

"Who's there?" Celia called out.

"We've come to see Mr. Lovejoy," was the answer.

"It is too late," she said and then whispered to Elijah, "I will tell them you are not here."

"No," Elijah said, putting his finger to her lips, calling out, "Yes, I am here. What do you want?"Asking again, "What do you want?" as he opened the door.

"We want you," one of the men said, reaching out to grab his shoulders, to force him from the house. Another man pulling on his nightshirt, while another hit him in the face.

"We want you. Traitor. Nigger lover. Liar."

Men with handkerchiefs over their faces. And more men behind them.

And then Celia. Her face white. Her voice shaking.

"Do not hurt him. Do not kill him," she said, shouting, hitting her fists wherever they might reach–a face, an arm, a back. "Do not... Do not..." she screamed. "Kill me first," she sobbed, clinging to her husband.

They left.

"Elijah Lovejoy will be killed within two weeks," they said.

One hundred fifty men with stones in their hands. Stones in their pockets. One hundred fifty men filling the street from the river to the warehouse.

One hundred fifty men throwing stones. No, it was more than 150 men—it was a mob.

Stones turning into rifles.

And in the background, between the shouts and the curses and the rifle shots—church bells started to ring loud and clear.

"Fire the warehouse."

"Burn them out."

"Shoot every damn abolitionist if they try to escape."

"What else could I do?" the woman asked. "There was nothing I could do, so I rang the church bells."

"Why are the church bells ringing so long, so late at night?" Celia Ann wondered.

She looked out the window. Snow was beginning to fall. Then the horse, coming down the street. Her husband's horse coming down the street with no one riding it.

"Tomorrow would have been his birthday," she said.

"An end," John said, "the end has come upon the four corners of the land. I will send mine anger upon thee, and will judge thee according to thy ways and will recompense upon thee all thy abominations. And mine eye shall not spare, neither will I have pity."

I closed my blouse. Put the baby down. Stirred the porridge. Porridge again for dinner. Porridge and potatoes.

"He's been murdered," John repeated. "The Presbyterian minister. The abolitionist. The editor of the Observer. Elijah Lovejoy," he said.

It was 1837.

Celia Ann Lovejoy had a son and was pregnant with a child who was dead. She was twenty-four years old. She was sick. She was frightened. She was poor. She was no longer beautiful. She was a widow. She returned to her parents' house. She moved to Cincinnati. She taught school. She worked as a seamstress. She tried to run a boardinghouse. She traveled to Canada.

"It's a place of freedom," she wrote her mother.

"Did you hear me?" John asked. "Elijah Lovejoy is dead. Murdered in cold blood. Murdered without a chance. Murdered defending freedom and justice, honor and God's salvation."

"Did you hear me?" John asked again, stopping briefly by Charles' cradle.

What was there to say?

I nodded. "Yes, I hear you," I said.

CHAPTER 13

"TWO MARES, TWO COWS, TWO HOGS, three lambs, nineteen hens, seven sheep, eleven Bibles, three pocket knives, two beds, one table, two chairs, your stew pot and fry pan, one washtub, one lantern, one plough, one axe and the old carriage. That's all we have," John said.

"That's all? That's all we have?" I asked.

John nodded.

I looked at the mud turtles the boys had caught.

"Salmon says he ate mud turtles once," Charles said as he put the bucket on the table.

"No, he didn't," Watson said.

"Yes, he did too," Charles insisted. "And besides you weren't there. Only Oliver and me were there. And they'll fry up real good. Salmon said so," he added, "and you don't even have to skin them."

"The tannery?" I asked John.

"Closed," he said.

"The race horses?" I asked.

"They've been taken for debt."

"The surveying at Oberlin College?"

"They've decided against it.".

"The sheep farm?"

"Just the seven sheep."

"The house?"

"We can stay through the winter."

"What will we do?"

"Pray and ask the Lord to fortify us for the trials ahead. Ask the Lord to show His mercy to us, to those who believe in Him and trust Him." He lowered his head. "Amen," he said.

A cool breeze blew through the window and whistled into the house.

"At least we have the cows," I said, pushing the cradle blanket into the washtub, squeezing it through the warm sudsy water. It was the blanket that I made for Sarah. I remember wanting it to have little pink and blue clouds on it, soft clouds, but I knew that was foolish and vain, so I made it a plain onion-skin yellow. Now it was frayed and the color of dirtied snow and smoke. Would I have time after I made curtains for the windows to make a new blanket or two? And shoes. Almost everyone needed shoes.

John was looking at me. I couldn't tell if he was unsettled with me or with himself. Looking at me. His eyes were shiny and hard as bone.

"For the babies," I explained. "I'm thinking of milk for the babies."

"Tut. Tut. Tut," he said, scratching his chin. "Do you think I've forgotten our babies? Must I remind you again and again that they are always deep in my thoughts? And do you think the Lord is not also mindful of them?"

"Of course the Lord is mindful. The Lord is the Lord..."

John interrupted. "If you are going to say 'the Lord is the Lord but...' don't say it. We cannot raise up God with one hand and pull Him down with the other. Do you understand?"

I knew if Johnny was here, he would have opened his Bible and read something that said the Lord is the Lord but... Then John would have opened his Bible and read something that said the Lord is the Lord from everlasting unto everlasting. Even if Owen and Jase were home and not gone out as farm hands, they would have talked back and forth—probably into the night. But I didn't know what else to say and now there was a quietness, a silence, except for Peter and Austin tumbling over each other like hungry puppies.

John scooped them up. "But there's good news," he said. "Captain Oviatt has hired me to overlook his sheep."

Peter wriggled. Austin started to cry.

John put the babies down. He turned toward me. A kind look, I thought. And then I thought that he might be coming closer to me, that he might put his arms around me. Not that he ever did that. And it's true I never thought about it before. That he would do that. That he would want to. That I would want him to, wanting him to come close because I wanted to know his strength. To feel it. That I needed his strength to touch mine. But he folded his arms across his chest.

"It will probably take a week or two, then I'll be taking a flock back east," he said.

"So soon?" I asked.

"The sooner the better," he said.

"Yes," I agreed. "I suppose the sooner the better."

And once again John started coming and going again, being in and out of my life. No, not really that. Never that. John was never out of my life. Never. He was in out of the house, but never out of my life.

"I arrived here four days ago, but shall probably leave soon," he wrote.

"I have not yet succeeded in my business, but think the prospect such that I do not by any means despair of final success," he wrote.

"Forgive the many faults and foibles you may have seen in me and try not any of you to get weary of well doing," he wrote.

"The time of my return is very uncertain, but will be soon as in any way consistent," he wrote.

"I hope God who is rich in mercy will grant us all grace to conform to our circumstances with cheerfulness and true resignation," he wrote.

"Try all of you to do the best you can, and do not one of you be discouraged, tomorrow may be a much brighter day," he wrote.

"May God in mercy keep us all, and enable us to get wisdom and with all our getting or losing to get understanding," he wrote.

"I want to see each of my dear family very much but must wait God's time," he wrote.

Letter by letter, day by day, time moving everything in its own way. In God's way.

In John's way.

And the summer that followed... That summer... The end of that summer...

Perhaps I should have known. But was it really so different from all other summers? True enough there was a drought and the fields and garden suffered. Sunflowers drooped, corn shriveled, there would be no pumpkins, hardly any tomatoes.

But the children... The children were growing and doing. I thought they were. There was no danger. I had no reason to think... How could I know? Of course, they had accidents and sicknesses, but sometimes I thought they were meant to be lessons–teaching them how to do something better, teaching them how to be stronger.

Day by day. The summer moving on toward winter.

First it was Frederick who was racing horses. He was a good rider but coming around the bend he was unseated, ,just missing the sharp edge of the fence, his head banging to the ground.

"Let me see," I said, taking his hands from his head.

There was redness but not much swelling.

"Your father has told you more times than flies buzzing on a carcass not to race those mares," I said. "Do you remember?"

"Yes, Mama," he said, his hands tight to his sides.

"It must be that the good Lord has more than one way of helping boys to remember," I said.

"Yes, Mama," he said.

I dug into the medicine box, found some burdock leaves, moistened them into a wad and put it to his head.

"Now don't go racing around. Just sit still and hold this on the sore spot."

"Yes, Mama," he said again.

Sarah came in with potatoes that she dug from the garden. She looked at Frederick. His head bent forward to his chest.

"Mama, is he going to die," she asked, looking up into his face.

"Since when does a bump in the head mean dying?" I said.

"Are you going to die?" she asked Frederick, coming a little closer to him.

Frederick didn't answer. Just keeping his hands, one over the other, tight to his head. Sitting like that a good long time until the redness began to clear and the swelling went down.

"It's alright, Frederick," I said. "It's going to be alright."

And it didn't seem to be anything that much, nothing more than a bump, but looking back, I think that was the beginning of those mean headaches that started to come on him and ready to lay him low.

And then there was that hot day, the hottest day at the end of a spell of hot days...

Ruth was going to make puff balls and Sarah wanted to fill them with blueberry jam.

"I think I'll go berry picking tomorrow," she said, "early tomorrow, so I can get to the hillside on the other side of town before it gets too hot."

"I'll go too," Watson said.

"Me too," Salmon said.

"And me," Charles said.

But in the morning after the boys finished stacking wood and weeding the garden, they wanted to go fishing.

"It's as sure as anything that it's a good morning for perch," Watson said.

"Well, I don't know about perch," Salmon said. "I have a feeling about bass this morning. A strong feeling about that."

"Me too," Charles said. "I'm going to catch a bass. A big bass. The biggest bass."

So Sarah went berry picking by herself.

"Don't get lost," I called after her. "And don't stay out too long in the sun."

"Don't worry, Mama. A girl who is ten years old, knows how to do things," she said.

"I'm thinking you're closer to nine," I reminded her, watching her set off, so sure and strong and sturdy.

But when Sarah came back from berry picking, her hands and arms were stuck all over with stickers.

"I didn't know blueberries grew on sticker bushes," I said, scraping her skin as gently as I could and pulling out the stickers.

"Don't worry, Mama," she said, as she held her breath. "My eyes are open and I'm not going to cry."

"Well, the worst is over and done with," I said, as I made a paste of vinegar, onion and parsley and put it to the red spots. "And you'll see it's not as troublesome as bee stings."

"And the berries," she asked, almost smiling, "can we save some for Papa?"

"Berries for Papa or for puffs?" I asked to tease her.

"Berries for Papa and for puffs," she said.

And then as I was thinking more about berries than worrying, and as I started to put the extra paste away, Charles came in. His trousers were rolled past his knees and his ankles were bloody with leech bites.

"But I almost got a bass," he said, "and it was so big it would have been enough for almost everyone. Almost everyone," he repeated, bending over his ankles and rubbing them.

"Rubbing is for washing clothes," I said. "Is that what you're doing?"

He hardly waited a minute. "No, Mama," he said, "because that's a joke and you can't do a joke, can you?"

"No, you can't," I said, as I put the rest of the paste to his legs.

And I think it was the same day. Yes, it was the same day that Austin fell from the swing Jase had knotted and hung. I heard him cry and a minute later Peter and Oliver raced into the house, not bothering to wipe their feet or close the door.

"Austin fell off the swing and broke his arm," Oliver said.

"Austin fell off the swing and broke his leg," Peter said.

"He did? And if he did, who is it walking through the door?" I asked.

"Mama, me fell," Austin said, big tears on his face.

I took him on my lap and wiped his face. "Even big boys have to hold on when they're swinging," I said, getting the camphor and bathing his arm with it. Then I tore small strips from the bottom of my bed sheet and carefully wound it around his arm up to his shoulder.

"See, it's as good as new," I said. "Now you keep it that

way."

"And you are the big boys," I said to Oliver and Peter, who were looking like statues, standing so still, "so you have to watch out for your little brother."

"Good as new. Good as new," Austin repeated. Then he turned to Oliver and Peter. "Want to swing?" he asked.

"Me first," Peter said.

"Okay," Oliver agreed. "I'll push."

And then, of course, there was the ague. You couldn't forget about that, but it was nothing special. Every family had it now and then. I remember when my father had it, shaking so much, he could hardly walk. He had to use a chamber pot and my mother only gave him liquids to eat. Feeding him, using the big spoon, but even so the liquid spilling off it, down into his beard. Raw egg, milk, soup, stew sauce.

When Owen and Jase came down with the ague, they were shaking too. Jase so much, I was afraid he would fall out of bed. But they could eat regular food and they took their pepper three times a day and they drank a trough-fill of the tea I steeped from mullein and marigold flowers.

The end of that summer. The heat finally broke. Cool breezes feathered the trees. Pine cones and acorns littered the forest floor. Squirrels were busy. Birds were on their journey south.

September.

That's what I thought. The seasons turning—as they always did, as they always would. God sitting up there in Heaven, turning his wheel slowly, smoothly. Humming maybe, like a spinning wheel. Round and round. As John said, "God in His wisdom. God in His Glory."

And then, one afternoon...

"Mama," I don't feel well," Charles said, coming in from the barn.

"Did you get all the eggs?" I asked.

He shook his head and coughed.

"Watson is bringing them in," he said.

"It's those leeches," I said, giving him a cup of tea and ground parsley. "Their bites can put poison in you for a long,

long time."

"Mama, I'm hot," he said a few minutes later, taking off his shirt.

"Drink the tea," I said, stirring in a little more parsley. "And it doesn't help that your hair is so long. Maybe after dinner Ruth will give it a short cut. That will give you some cooling."

"Mama, I'm cold," he said a few minutes later, hugging himself. Shivering.

I put his shirt back on and buttoned the buttons.

"Once the summer is over, nights can cool down quickly," I said. "Just look at me, I'm shivering myself."

He coughed again. He started to cry.

Six years old. My bravest one. That time when the sheep got out of their pen, he was the one who went with Owen and Jase to find them. Out all night—and a dark night it was, with no moon. Then coming home by himself because he had gotten separated from his brothers.

"I wasn't afraid," he said. He made a muscle. "Look at my muscle. See I'm strong. And I'm brave."

Coughing. Shivering. And crying.

Dinner time and Charles went to bed. Jase brought him warm dumplings. Ruth went with a cup of bread pudding. Sarah carried the big black berries that were so sweet. But he ate nothing.

"Is he very sick?" Sarah asked.

"No, he's not very sick," I said. "Just sick. Plain sick. It's likely he caught the ague from Jase or Owen. He's always trailing after them, following them around. And that's how it goes, from one to another."

I warmed some milk and beat a raw egg into it.

Owen was rubbing his sore arm with a new battery machine.

Frederick was quiet. It looked like one of his headaches was beginning.

"Now you have to drink this," I said to Charles.

He opened his mouth. He swallowed once. Twice. Three times. Then he coughed and cried again.

I pulled the blanket up to his chin.

Oliver came in. He was carrying the lamb Jase had carved for him the time he ate a fistful of sumac leaves and almost died. Oliver put the lamb next to Charles, close to his side.

The clang of dishes.

Ruth and Jase were clearing and washing. Owen was mopping.

I could feel the new baby kick inside me. Turn over. I shivered. I thought I was going to be sick.

I opened the front door.

"I'm doing a little poorly myself," I said. "Sarah, you will have to take care of the little ones."

Sarah nodded. She liked taking care of the little ones. "I can be their pretend mother," she would say. And she would sing them a psalm. Maybe teach them a new one. "So we can surprise Papa," she said.

"But not me," Oliver protested. "I'm not a little one."

Peter wrinkling his nose. "I'm a little one," he said.

"Me too," Austin said.

It was the first time I was sick and didn't finish my chores. The first time I turned from the children and took to bed.

That night I dreamed about Charles and the new baby. Charles was trying to cover the baby, but the baby was kicking and turning. Then the baby was big. Bigger than Charles. "I don't want that blanket," the baby said. "I want my own blanket." And the baby kept on getting bigger and bigger, its head up against the sky. A pink and blue sky, almost like a sunset but it was barely noon.

In the morning Charles was no better. In the afternoon he was no better. In the evening there were white spots in his mouth. The next day there were more white spots, turning gray. The next day I called Dr. Selman. The spots were bigger and turning black.

Dr. Selman shook his head. He opened his bag and took out a small knife.

"Hold his mouth open," he said.

I pressed my fingers against his cheeks, pushing between his teeth, opening his mouth.

"Wider," the doctor said.

I pushed harder.

And then there was blood. Bubbles of blood.

"I'm cutting some of the blisters," the doctor said, "but it may be too late." He closed his bag. "We'll see what happens tomorrow."

In the morning Charles was no better. In the afternoon he was no better. In the evening the spots in his mouth were bigger. Blacker.

Dr. Selman came again.

"Hold his mouth open," he said.

Once again I pressed my fingers against his cheeks, pushing between his teeth, opening his mouth.

"Wider," the doctor said.

Again I pushed harder.

The doctor shook his head.

"Keep him warm and comfortable," he said. "That's all we can do. The rest is up to our Maker."

We prayed. That evening, well into the night, we all prayed. On and off. Sometimes together. Sometimes alone. Sometimes silently.

The next day Charles was sleeping more. Waking only to cough. Waking only to try to catch his breath. And even when he did, he kept his eyes closed and said nothing.

The next day Charles did not wake.

CHAPTER 14

COFFINS. NO, A COFFIN. One coffin. At first, just one.

Owen and Jase planing the boards. Sawing them. Hammering–so much hammering.

Ruth measuring and sewing, fixing the lining for the coffin from her new calico skirt.

Frederick measuring the coffin, digging into the earth.

Sarah edging the coffin with blue star flowers.

Salmon and Watson carving a little headstone.

Oliver giving his lamb, putting it in a dip in the sheet that covered Charles. "He can hold it later, can't he, Mama?" he asked, not waiting for an answer.

Peter picking up the sheet, touching the hand. "Mama, he's cold," he said. "Mama, he's very cold."

"He's not cold," I said as firmly as I could.

Austin asking for a push on the swing. "Now Cheese," he said because he couldn't say Charles. "Cheese, get up and push..."

I was washing his clothes. I stopped for a minute. Felt the baby inside me. Looked out the window. Saw the clouds in the sky. Gray. Gray as wolves. They looked like wolves.

"I told you before to leave your brother alone," I said. "He's gone, gone all the way up to Heaven. He's living with angels."

"Is he playing with them?" Peter asked.

"Yes, he's playing with them," I said.

Sarah came in. "I'll take them out," she said. And Peter and Austin marched after her singing, Onward Christian Soldiers...

Then everything was done. It was over.

Jase and Owen put Charles in the coffin. Frederick shoveled the earth. Sarah was still singing Onward Christian Soldiers. Oliver was clinging to Ruth. I was holding Austin. Peter was tugging at my skirt.

"Might just as well write to your father that it's all over," I told Jase. "No need for him to come home now."

Coming home from the cemetery. Gathering around the table that Aunt Fannie had set. Food that would make your mouth water if your tongue wasn't so stiff and dry. So very dry.

Jase bowed his head. Folded his hands in front of him.

"I will not be lengthy," he said. "The Judge of all the earth has done and will do right. Let us give glory and honor and power and thanks unto Him that sitteth on the throne forever and ever. Amen."

"Amen," we all said.

I felt a heaviness. I shivered.

Sarah coughed.

Peter couldn't seem to catch his breath.

Austin started to cry.

One week later Peter was dead.

The next day Sarah said, "I will meet God in Paradise..."

And then Austin. So little. So very little...

And it's true. That's when I saw a rainbow.

CHAPTER 15

"I WILL NOT GO. NO, I WILL NOT GO."

John frowned.

"I have never said no. I do not want to say no, but I cannot go," I said. "I cannot leave them."

Still frowning. His eyebrows coming together. His hands clasping and unclasping in front of him.

"And I suppose you think they are in that little cemetery, in the ground?" he finally said. "I suppose you think a box is strong enough to hold them, that their souls are buried in the dirt with the worms? Is that what you think? That God has no pity? No power? No plan?"

I thought I might cry. I never cried. I felt too hard to cry. Too tired to cry. Maybe too old or too small...

"Have you forgotten that our true home is in Heaven? That our true and kind and merciful Father is in Heaven and awaits us? That he welcomes our souls?"

The baby cried. Little Annie–covered with the frayed onion-skin yellow blanket. I turned to her, unbuttoning my blouse.

It was a new house, I remember that. A good house. A very good house.

Could the children look down from Heaven and see it? All the rooms with proper doors? The sturdy windows, facing east to the sun? The large garden? The ample yard? The way the house sat on a little hill and the way you could see so far? Would they know the school was near-by? Would they know there was trout in the streams that often crisscrossed into each other? Would they know that sometimes we had fresh biscuits for breakfast and dinner? That everyone had new Sunday clothes?

Would the children know that we moved to Akron?

So John was a partner once again. Shepherd to Mr. Perkins' flock of 1,500 Saxony sheep.

"What about this wool?" he was asked.

"It's a good grade from Ohio," he said.

"And the origin of this wool?"

"It's a middle grade from Vermont."

"And this wool?"

"Gentlemen," John said feeling the sample carefully and smiling. "Gentlemen, If you have any machinery that will work up dog's hair, I would advise you to put this into it."

John was buying sheep. Herding them. Staying up all night to nurse a sick lamb, bathing it in warm water, feeding it warm milk with a teaspoon. Sometimes selling a lamb for $100. Selling wool. Representing other wool growers. Traveling between the sheep farmers in Ohio and the wool manufacturers in New England. Opening his office in Springfield, Massachusetts. Traveling from Akron to Cleveland. From Akron to Springfield. Traveling and writing.

"I would you should realize that, notwithstanding I am absent in body, I am very much of the time present in spirit," he wrote.

"I do not forget the firm attachment of her who has remained my fast and faithful affectionate friend, when others said of me, 'Now that he lieth, he shall rise up no more...'" he wrote.

"I want your face to shine, even if my own should be dark and cloudy," he wrote.

"After being so much away, it seems as if I knew pretty well how to appreciate the quiet of home. There is a peculiar music in the word which a half-year's absence in a distant country would enable you to understand," he wrote.

"I now feel encouraged to believe that my absence will not be very long," he wrote.

Prudence Crandall was also traveling. A woman alone, a woman leaving her husband, his house.

"I forbid you to be reading books," he said.

"Why?" she asked.

"Because there's nothing more you need to know," he said.

"Why?" she asked.

"Because you know as much as a woman should..."

Prudence Crandall Philleo. Mrs. Philleo, traveling fifteen hundred miles to Illinois to work the Crandall homestead. She fixed up the house and added a fence. She did a large haying and got in fifty acres of wheat and oats. She raised the corn house up on staves to keep out the rats. She covered the potatoes with horse dung to keep them from freezing.

Sometimes her neighbors helped. Other times her neighbors thought it wasn't God's way for a woman to be doing a man's work.

"But how can it be a man's work if I'm doing it?" she said more than once. "And it's my land and my work," she added.

And sometimes she said, "Man's work. Woman's work. What's the difference? I've left my husband, was that woman's work?"

About the same time Sojourner Truth asked, "Is God dead?"

Harriet Beecher Stowe was thinking of writing a book about slavery.

And Lucy Stone. Have you heard of Lucy Stone?

And in my household, after Annie came Amelia. John called her "Little Chick."

CHAPTER 16

SEPTEMBER AGAIN.

Ruth came home to help.

Looking out the window with the baby in my arms.

"What will we name the baby?" John had asked.

"Sarah," I said. "It has to be Sarah. Nothing else."

"Sarah, of course," he agreed.

Watching her. I see her walking up the street with the step of a young woman. She is a young woman—as young as I was when I made my way through the forest. That day, that cold day, never guessing where my life was going, how it would change.

Closer to the house.

Warm for September. The uproar of tree frogs and katydids. The thinning shadows of trees. A maple leaf twirling about her head. She reaches for it. She catches it. A red one. And then a leaf, both yellow and red.

And then she is home.

"Isn't it something, after so many boys all of a sudden we have girls in the family," she began, as she took off her bonnet. "Let me see her. Oh my, so small. And so pink and fair. Was Sarah..." She stopped. "I'm sorry," she said. "Did I start you thinking about the Sarah we lost?"

Did I nod? I think so, walking slowly through the kitchen, the dishes piled in the tub because the older boys were working in the field and Oliver was minding Annie and Amelia.

Slowly to the front room, the parlor, which had become my bedroom.

"I am tired," I said, getting into bed, keeping the baby to my side.

My head sank into the pillow. I closed my eyes. Opened them. It was hard to open them. To keep them open.

"It's just that I can see her," I said. "I can see her so plain. And Charles, so eager to do like a man. And the babies..."

Ruth sat on the edge of the bed. She raised her hands. Her fingertips coming together as if she might start to pray.

I waited. I wanted to tell her it was good to have her home. That in a way, she was my first little girl...

"That's a fine looking bonnet you have," I said. "It looks just right with your eyes."

"Do you think so?" She seemed surprised.

"It's fine to have blue eyes. Really fine."

"Well," she said, almost laughing, a small laugh, "the eyes are mine but I borrowed the bonnet from Eva."

"Eva?"

"A school friend. A good school friend," she said, letting the words school and friend and good drift in the space between us. Hang there. "A black girl..."

"A black girl with blue eyes?"

"But she's not really black. She's more like field color, like when the field is plowed in the spring. Sometimes when I see her I also see rabbits hopping in front of the machines, birds following behind."

And then in a louder voice, almost stern, she asked, "Mama, do you know what we do in school?"

"Of course, I know what you do. You study. You learn. You could be a teacher..."

"Yes, we do that, but we also talk. Sometimes we talk late into the night. Sometimes when we are talking, we can see the stars fade into morning."

"Talking, just talking the whole night away. It must be important," I said, catching a mosquito on the back of my neck, a drop of blood on my finger.

I sat up. I touched her shoulder.

"Do you talk about slavery? If it's about slavery, you must be careful. There's danger in that kind of talk. Did you tell your father? He can help. And Johnny and Jase and Owen... We promised... I promised..."

"Mama, don't get so excited." She reached for my hand, holding it in hers for a moment. "We don't need help. We're not doing anything. We're just talking. Just girls talking. That's what I wanted to tell you. Just girls talking."

"Just girls?"

She nodded.

"Frivolous talk?" I asked. "Gossip?"

"I don't think so. Would I be talking frivolous? Godless?"

She shook her head. Frowning, so much like John I expected to hear her say Tut, tut, tut.

"Once," she almost whispered, as if she was telling me a secret, "I asked her how it felt for a black girl to have blue eyes. Once she asked me if it was hard coming up without a mother."

I caught my breath.

Coming up without a mother? But that's not the way it was, I wanted to say. You had a mother. Always. Every day. And if I wasn't your mother from the beginning, I was still your mother.

"I was your mother..." I began.

Ruth took my hands.

"Yes, of course, that's what I said, that I had a mother coming up—and even now."

I fingered the edge of the blanket. A new one for little Sarah, the new Sarah, the second Sarah. It was raspberry color. From the berries Ruth had picked, sorted, strained, boiled down, thickened.

"Talking. Just talking," I repeated.

She nodded.

"And sometimes it feels good. Like a stone is lifted from your back or blinders from your eyes. Did you ever feel that way?"

I tried to think back to talking. Back to feeling good and talking. But talking was always so hard. So extra. Wondering what to say and the worry that you would say the wrong thing.

"I don't know. Maybe with my sister once or twice. She was the good talker. The good thinker too. And she was quick and smart. She could have been a teacher. Yes, I think she could have been a teacher. I know it—and then she died so suddenly..."

Ruth lowered her voice.

"Mama," she said, "there's so much to remember, so much—and so much to talk about. And we are talking. You are talking and I am talking. Mother and daughter talk. Almost girl talk."

There was a silence. An open silence, a silence that was opening. Not a hole. Not a trap. A door. A simple door.

"She could have been your mama," I whispered. "She was almost..."

The door closed. Swung shut.

Did Ruth hear me? Did she know? Did she know that my sister died of a broken heart?

She didn't answer. She was playing with Sarah. She touched her forehead. Her cheek. Her lips.

"Do you know what I think?" she asked.

"What?"

"When I think of our first Sarah I think of something lucky. Something lucky that came to us..."

She hesitated. Then continued.

"Do you know what I remember?"

"What?"

"I remember those little yellow birds when we lived in Randolph. They looked like dandelions, dandelions that could fly. And I thought if I was good, they could bring us good luck. I thought..."

"But Ruth you were always good and helping. You were..."

She smiled.

"I know, not too many trips to the barn. But I hoped and prayed and I thought if I could get the birds to sing on Mama's grave, she would wake up and be alive again. I used to pray to God, I used to ask Him to let them sing, to make them sing... Just once..."

"You were hurting?"

"I didn't tell anyone. I thought I was bad because Mama was in Heaven and it wasn't right to make her come back to earth. And I was praying and praying for God to make me good. And now do you know what I think?" she asked.

"What?"

"I think that when you lose something, maybe someone

else finds it. Maybe someone who needs it more. And that means it's not really lost, so you didn't lose it. Even if you don't have it, you didn't lose it. Eva said that to me once. She said, 'You know you can lose something and still have it.'"

"What did Eva lose?" I asked.

"A sister, the same age as Sarah, killed by horses..." she began.

Then we heard doors and drawers opening and closing in the kitchen.

Ruth got up.

"You stay in bed and take care of little Sarah," she said. "I'll be fixing dinner."

I closed my eyes. The sun was breaking into colors, stitches of color darting here and there. If they only held still, came together, they could have been something pretty. Maybe even a rainbow.

It didn't take long. A few days. I was feeling stronger. Bread was baking. Pies were cooking. Beef was cured. We started harvesting the garden. I started the drying and canning. Ruth started the weaving and mending. We cleaned the kitchen from floor to rafters. We filled in the window cracks. We fixed the step on the front porch.

And then it was Monday. A good clear sunny breezy Monday.

"Clothes will dry as quick as we can hang them," I said.

"Save the neighbors the pester of smelling us before they see us," Ruth said, heating water for the tub, sorting the clothes into piles.

Annie went with Oliver looking for mushrooms that we could pickle.

Amelia stayed home, sitting on one pile of clothes, then the other. Hopping from one to the other. Picking up clothes. Holding them against her. Trying to fit into anything big—Oliver's shirt, Watson's britches, Salmon's vest, even Frederick's socks, my petticoat.

"Yook at me. Yook at me, Tuth," she called.

"You're messing up the piles, but you are funny," Ruth said, pouring the hot water from the pots to the tub.

Steam from the water curled the loose hair on Ruth's forehead and the back of her neck. Amelia's hair was still soft and thin, baby fuzz, not enough of it to curl.

Little Sarah was sleeping.

"I'll bring in the apples and pears," I said, walking out the door. Thinking... was it the first time I walked out the door with no baby in my arms? With no one holding onto my skirt? No one following?

I did not hurry. Pulling down the branches, filling the bushel. I could hear the chopping of wood, the clearing of fields. The sheep on the hillside moving so slowly, they looked like nothing more than pictures pasted on the grass.

Suddenly Ruth was there. She took one handle of the bushel, waited for me to pull up on the other. Then we started back to the house.

A scream.

I don't know if we heard a scream. Maybe we did. Maybe we had to hear a scream because I remember dropping the bushel, just letting it go. Dropping it. And I remember the apples and pears rolling to the ground. Slowly it seemed. And we had to step over them. Each one. So many apples and pears. And then we ran to the house...

No.

If there had been a scream I think I would remember it. I would still hear it. A call, "Mama. Mama." And I can't hear it. But I can still see her. Her little body. Red. Scorched. Stretched in some places. Twisted in others. Blisters bubbling up. Her eyes rolling up, hiding inside themselves, inside a blister.

No.

There was no scream. How could there be? The way her

lips were stuck together, bubbled together. Her nose, her little nose also stuck together so she couldn't breathe.

Yes, there was a scream. My scream. I screamed.

"Make a poultice. Make a poultice."

And I tried to open her mouth. Her nose. The skin of her nose peeling, coming off into my hand.

Once again Frederick digging into the earth. Ruth lining the coffin. Watson and Salmon carving a headstone, trying to fashion a small chick on it. Once again I was standing at the edge of a grave. Little Sarah sleeping in my arms. Annie on one side. Oliver, rocking back and forth, on my other side.

Once again a letter to John.

And John's letter.

"I returned after an absence of several days and am utterly unable to give any expression of my feelings on hearing of the dreadful news. I seem to be struck almost dumb. One more dear little feeble child I am to meet no more till the dead small and great shall stand before God. This is a bitter cup indeed, but blessed be God—a brighter day shall dawn; and let us not sorrow as those that have no hope. But Divine Providence does seem to lay a heavy burden and responsibility on you my dear Mary... "

CHAPTER 17

RED.

The color red. Just plain red. It was becoming my favorite color. I would have served red porridge if I could, red eggs, red milk, red chicken, red corn, red peas, red pumpkin, red soup...

Red.

Bright red. Creeping over everything. Coloring it. Casting a red shadow. Did you ever see a red table? A red garden? A red church? Did you ever see red rain falling into a red river? And, at night, red stars? Did you ever see children with red faces and red hands wearing red coats? Whose children were they? Where did they come from? Where were they going? Were they black children trying to be white? White children pretending to be black? Were they my children. Which ones? Which ones were they? Which ones would they be?

Red.

As red as a rainbow whose only color is red. As sharp as a knife. As stiff as a man. Slicing into the body of a red woman. Until she breaks or folds.

"Again?" I asked.

"Living in Springfield will be good," John said. "The warehouse is a few streets away. The office is a few streets away. And," he lowered his voice, "people there are doing what needs to be done. People we can talk to. People who can help us with our plan."

He began looking at things. The clothes. The furniture. The dishes in the cupboard. The pots and pans. The tubs. The books.

He stopped.

"What do you think, should we buy a new bed?" he asked.

"No," I said, "the bed is still sturdy and strong."

"Maybe we should get a bigger sideboard?"

"No," I said. "A side-board is not flesh and blood, It is not right or wrong. It is not as important as our plan."

"A set of tableware?"

"No," I said. "Our plan is our plan and whatever money we have is ours to fight slavery."

So we traveled to Springfield. The nine of us. Two wagons taking us to the train station. The boys piling up our boxes and bundles. Waiting. Peering down the tracks and into the distance. Salmon and Watson so close to the edge. Thinking they were too close to the edge. My sons. Watson, almost as good a sheepherder as Jase or Owen, and Salmon learning fast. Almost calling, Watson, Salmon, watch out, you're too close. The tracks, smooth and silvery as ice.

"This way. This way," John was saying as he led us forward.

Watson and Salmon right behind him. Salmon so tight he came near to pushing John once or twice. Annie holding John's hand and Ruth holding her other hand. Oliver staying back with me. "So you don't get lost, Mama," he said. Frederick a few steps off to the side.

Then the whistle of the train, like wind screaming in front of a storm. Even little Sarah stopped crying.

Space and time. I talked about that before, didn't I? But now I felt as if space and time weren't out there someplace, but inside the storm. Inside the train. Inside us. And it seemed as if there was so much of both–and then again so little. And it seemed as if only the storm was real and we were real only because we were in it. Everything tumbling together, mixing together. And there was no stopping. No place to stop and rest. Passing over. Passing through. So quickly. A hill here. A hill there. A farm. A field. A meadow. Crossing a river. Traveling through one town. Two towns. Three. Puffs of black smoke.

And the whistle blowing day or night.

So strange. As if I was there and wasn't there. Like a dream and I would awaken. But where? Where would I be?

"We're here," John finally said, as the train slowed. "This is it. This is Springfield."

The train's whistle blew. Its wheels screeched. It pulled forward. It stopped. It pulled forward again.

"This is it," John repeated, lifting Annie so she could have a better look from the window. "And there, exactly right there, is the Perkins and Brown warehouse."

"Where? Where?" Annie asked, trying to follow the line of his pointing finger.

John held her a little higher. "Look there, just behind the stable and the tavern. Now to the right a little."

"I see it. I see it," Oliver said, jumping up and down. "It's so big. I didn't know it was so big." Still jumping, he raised his arms as far as they would go over his head. "So big. This big. So big," he said.

"It's the biggest," John said. "And it's filled to the rafters with good Saxony sheep wool."

"Mr. Perkins says it's the best wool in the whole country," Watson said.

John was pleased. He put Annie down.

"Son," he said, almost shaking Watson's hand, "it would make no more sense to argue with Mr. Perkins than with the man in the moon."

He turned to me.

"Mary, do you see it?" he asked. "Do you see the warehouse?"

He took Sarah from my arms.

"Look," he said, pointing with his finger again.

I looked.

"Yes," I said.

I thought I saw it. I saw the tavern. The stable. The church. And then the large building. That must be it. The largest building I had ever seen.

Ruth stood up. She opened the window.

"Look, there's Johnny. Johnny," she called, waving to him.

"And, by the wagons, there's Jase and Owen," Salmon said.

"So we're all here," John said, looking at us, returning Sarah to my arms. "Let us not forget this feeling, this joy, this thankfulness. And at the same time let us remember that other families are now, even as we stand here together, being torn apart. Separated, not by God, but by man, for the reason of greed. The only reason. As if the world to come had no judge and no justice." He shook his head in sorrow. "Babies torn from their mothers. Children from their parents. Parents from each other. But as we have been blessed, we must always remember to thank the good Lord and to share the blessing as best we can."

He stood up. We stood up, reaching for the little packages to take with us.

"This way. This way," he said once again, leading us forward. Slowly forward.

Nine months later Ellen was born and John came home from the warehouse to heat the water, get the doctor, and wrap the baby in Sarah's raspberry blanket.

CHAPTER 18

"WAR IS WAR AND KILLING IS KILLING," Frederick Douglass said.

"Are you serious? How can you be serious?" John asked. "This is not a classroom. The world is not a school. How can you think that anything of worth is that simple?"

"Isn't right and wrong simple?"

John hesitated for a moment.

"You do have a way with words," he said. "You can take a phrase from an angel and hand it over to the devil as if they were brothers living side by side."

"I can say what I say because I believe what I say."

"And so do I," John said. "And so do I. That's why I can say that this war with Mexico is folly. It is and will bring no good. Mark my words, that war will be a boon and boost for slavery throughout the country."

John spoke a little louder. A little faster. The lines in his face deep and dark.

"So I can say, with the Lord as my witness, that some wars are perfidious. They address no evil and they right no wrong. But the war against slavery..."

"The war?"

"If there were to be a war, that war would be just because the sin is great and there is no other way." He looked directly at Mr. Douglass. "We must work together, Frederick. We must be prepared to give our all, to die if need be..."

"Thou shalt not kill."

"An eye for an eye."

"An eye for an eye," Mr. Douglass repeated after a few

moments. "Yes, you may be right, John. It may come down to that."

Oliver cleared the table. Salmon scraped scraps into the bucket. Ruth piled the dishes, soaked them and began to wash.

I watched. Sitting and watching. Wondering why I was just sitting and watching—for a second or two and then Ellen started to cry.

"The baby," Watson said. "I'll get her."

"No, me. I'll get her," Salmon said, letting beef scraps and grease fall to the floor.

"Tut, tut, tut," John began. "Do you think two boys are needed to get one baby?"

"No, sir," Watson said. "But I was first."

John looked at Salmon.

"No, sir," he said.

"But two boys can wash a floor that needs washing," John continued. "Can't they?"

"Yes, sir," Watson said.

"Yes, sir," Salmon said.

Annie was washing Sarah's hands and face.

"Mama, look how dirty she is. She looks like a devil."

Sarah started to cry. "No devil. No devil," she said.

Oliver left the table and reached behind Annie. He flipped her braids up and down. "You don't have to worry about a devil. You don't even have to think about a devil," he said. "There's no devil in this house. Never was and never will be."

"Well, anyway, she's got potato in her hair."

I stood up.

"It's the baby," I said, turning to John and Mr. Douglass. "She has a way of knowing when we've eaten and now she thinks it's her turn."

John nodded.

Mr. Douglass rose from his chair, tipped his head politely.

It was summer. A warm day and little Ellen, pale and fuzzy, was warm in my arms. A dusting of crushed dock root did not cover the heat rash on her neck and face.

I went to the bedroom, sat down on the Mama Chair, with arms to support my arms and a strong solid back that felt good against mine.

Little cries becoming big cries...

"Yes, yes, yes, little Ellen," I said, almost saying little Sarah, little Charles, little Peter, little Austin, little Amelia. Babies. All my little babies.

"Little Ellen, little Ellen," I said again, opening my blouse, giving her my breast. Waiting until she took hold. Hard and tight. One suck, two sucks. Waiting. Holding my breath. Waiting. And then as it did the last time and the time before that, the crack in my nipple opening. I took a deep breath. I bit my lip. Pains circled my chest, crowded into my throat and up into my head.

I pulled back. She held on. I wanted to close my eyes. I wanted to go to sleep. Another baby... Another baby... Another baby...

I cried.

I prayed.

"Dear God, let me be strong one more time. This time. This baby."

I pulled back again, pressing my fingers into her mouth. Opening her mouth. Pulling free. The pain in my head like fence wire. Barbed wire.

"Little Ellen, little Ellen, what are we going to do?" I said, shifting her to my other side.

She opened her eyes. Eyes as clear as honey. She sucked for a little while, her breathing calm and peaceful, her fingers curling around mine, the blood on my finger, just a drop, so big on hers. Slowly, quietly sucking, falling asleep.

So many things can bring you to the edge of thinking, the edge of knowing. A little baby bringing its own edge. On one side life. On the other side death.

"She's sleeping," I said to Ruth, as I put her back in the cradle. "But it's true, as true as we're standing here..."

A pause.

"What's true?" Ruth asked.

"That even good cows can get old, can get too old."

Another pause. A whippoorwill calling into it.

"Who's a cow?" she asked, pretending that she was looking

around. "Where's a cow? Do you see a cow? I don't see any cows."

"But I can only give her one side and it can't be enough. I'm afraid... She's always hungry—don't you think so? Her face is round but her arms and legs are thin. And sometimes she spits up blood."

"Blood? Is she bleeding?"

"No, she's not bleeding."

"Are you bleeding?"

I nodded. "It's my blood. And sometimes when the crack opens, she sucks blood and then she spits it up."

Ellen started fussing.

"See? Do you hear her? She's hungry again.

"Maybe not. Maybe she's just settling down." Ruth took a towel and dried her hands. Then she put her arm on my shoulder and around my back. Long arms. I wanted to say Ruth, you have very good long arms.

"You know what?" she continued. "You're just like a new mother, not an old cow."

"Maybe," I said. "Maybe she's just settling down. But maybe I should give her something else, something more. Maybe I should give her some strained oats or flour water or soup broth."

The kitchen. A small room. Looking around. Suddenly seeing how small it was. Yes, it was good we didn't buy a bigger sideboard.

Just Ruth and me. Just Ruth—Dianthe's daughter and mine—and me. Just two women in the kitchen. Three? Was Dianthe there? To see her daughter? Her only daughter. The daughter we shared...

Ruth was rinsing the soap from the pots and pans.

"All through for tonight," she said.

I looked at Ellen. Her eyes were closed. Her lips almost coming to a smile. But she would waken soon. How soon? In an hour? Two hours? And she would cry and scream and gasp until I fed her. Again. All through the night.

I rocked the cradle.

I was thinking of John and Mr. Douglass. After dinner they had gone to meet with Mr. Smith.

"He is the key to our plan,' John said. "I'm sure of it."

For money? For guns? John didn't say. Maybe he didn't know.

I looked at Ruth. I could see her standing in a schoolroom, writing on a chalkboard, telling a story, reading a prayer, showing directions on a map. Or would she be standing in front of a sink, a stove, a washtub? Choices. Ruth was young. She was strong. She was smart and she had choices. Did she know that? Did she know that she was lucky? That she could claim some part of her life, of her time, for herself? Girl talk? Yes, even for frivolous girl talk.

Suddenly I asked, "Do you think there will be a war to free the slaves?"

Ruth had started to brush her hair. She stopped. I stopped rocking the cradle. We looked at each other. I think I was as much surprised as she was.

She started brushing her hair again. Slowly. Long slow sweeps of her hand. Long slow sweeps of her hair.

"It's already a war," she answered. "The difference is that only one side is getting killed. Murdered. Slaughtered. Only one side. Always the same side. And the women and children... Our sheep get better care."

"So we have to give the other side guns and whips? And then it will be the side that does the most killing that wins?"

Ruth frowned. "There can only be one winner," she said. "One heaven. One hell. One God and one winner."

"Yes, yes, of course," I agreed, starting to rock the cradle again, harder than before, "But do you think your father will fight?"

"Father is already fighting."

"Yes, yes, of course, but what I mean is–do you think he will kill?"

I stopped rocking the cradle. It was the wrong time to talk about war and killing. It was late. I was tired. Ruth was going out. War and killing–you needed time to talk about that, time to even think about that. Not just to snatch at it, little bits and pieces of it here and there.

Ruth put her hair up with one of those pretty combs.

The three little ones burst into the room.

"Annie almost got caught in the wheel of a wagon," Oliver said, "but I saved her."

"And Sarah fell into a ditch. She really did, honestly," Annie said, "but I saved her."

"Full of mud. The three of you. That's what you are..." I began.

Ruth interrupted. "Walking mud pies," she said, pointing them to the bedroom. "And leave the muddy clothes on the floor."

"Me too?" Oliver asked.

"You too," she said

Ruth turned from them to me. Her eyes so blue. Just like John's. No, bluer. Her eyes were bluer than his.

"I don't know," she said softly. "I don't know."

CHAPTER 19

"I DON'T KNOW," I SAID. Was I wringing my hands? I think so.

"We have no choice. This is not a time for choosing, for stopping, for going back. We are coming close to action. To do what needs to be done. To remember our pledge. To remember our plan. To work. To fight. To attack the colossal wrong. To win. To win, Mary. To win. We must win."

"I know," I said again, "but I just don't know."

"Mary," he said, his eyes wide and sharp, as if he was seeing more than he was seeing. "You are not making any sense."

"I know," I said.

I took a deep breath.

"I can't leave her. 'Mama,' she said, "and I still hear her calling, 'Mama, Mama.' And I held her..."

"Do you think my love was less than yours? Didn't I hold her? Didn't I rock her? Do you think she wasn't in my heart as well? She was my kitten, my little kitten..."

"So gray. She got so gray. Not even one year on this earth and she looked so wasted and old."

John turned away from me. Once his back was square and straight, now his shoulders sloped into his side.

"It's not for us to question God." His words drifted to me from across a distance, almost like an echo. "We are servants. Only that."

"I'm not questioning. I'm not arguing. I'm not doubting. I just can't put another baby in the ground and move away."

"But we must do what we must do and we must move where we must move. And the time is now."

"I just don't know. I just can't do it."

"Mary, you must know. You must understand. It is not as if we were leaving her and rushing away to search for gold or to seek some worldly pleasure or profit. It is not as if we were turning from our obligations and our duties. Exactly the opposite is true. It is not the gold of this life that we are committed to. It is the everlasting gold of God's word. God's purpose is our goal and our gold. Our service to Him is our reward."

"She was wrinkled. Even the shadows about her were wrinkled. And she was afraid. I know she was afraid. I think she was afraid to close her eyes..."

"Mary, where is our little Ellen? Where do you think she is?"

"She is in Heaven and she is beautiful."

"Then we will go," John said.

It was the beginning of the pledge. Maybe not the beginning of battles and bloodshed, but the beginning of the plan.

How many days? I don't remember how many days.

"Timbucto?" Ruth asked.

"Timbucto," John answered.

Bumping along, north, to mountains and forests. Through mountains and forests. Around them. North, where there was nothing. Nothing that I could see. A cold, bone-chilling rain. I bundled Annie in sweaters, rolled Sarah in blankets.

"Smell the air," John said. "It's strong and clean."

He stopped the wagon. "Drink the water," he said, cupping his hands in the rushing stream. "It's clear and cold."

"And look at the view. So many evergreens the world will look green even in winter," he said.

"Yes," Ruth finally answered. "Yes, the view is certainly grand."

And the house?

"The house is small," John said. "But we are here and the main thing is for us to remember our plan and keep good natured."

And then a knock on the door.

A man standing there. So big he darkened the sun behind

him. So dark, the whites of his eyes shone like moons. And his hands—maybe that's what I remember most, his hands—opening and closing. Still as a fence post, his hands opening and closing.

Was it a sign? I thought so. The very first morning we were there, God guiding this black man's footsteps to our door.

"Come in," I said. "You are welcome."

Suddenly John was at my side.

"Come in, come in," he said, taking the man's arm. "Have you traveled far?"

The man hesitated.

"It is alright," John said. "We are abolitionists and you are safe here."

"I've come from Florida," the man said, looking around, his hands opening and closing.

Oliver came to the door. "How did you get here?" he asked.

"I walked," the man said.

"Walked?" I repeated, looking at his feet.

"In the winter, did you walk through the ice and snow?" Ruth asked.

The man nodded, not looking at anyone.

"But it is over," John said. "Your sojourn is over. By the grace of God you have found us and you will stay here with us."

The man spoke in a low voice, almost a whisper. "I'm a slave," he said.

"Not anymore," John said, taking him into the room, patting him on the back, giving him a chair at the table.

And that's the way it was, the way John said it would be. The way he said our plan would work. That black men would come and we would help them to live on the land, to sustain themselves, to work hard and be free. It was as John said, "If you open your heart you can see angels."

But it wasn't easy. The earth wasn't easy or giving. Not like Pennsylvania and worse than Ohio. The earth was hard. Frozen so much of the time. And rocks. Wherever you went to put in a shovel or a plough, there was the ringing sound of rocks.

"A rock is a rock and a man is a man," John said, "and a man is stronger than a rock and a man is better than a rock and a man will prevail."

So we planted as much as we could. Everyone helping—Ruth, Frederick, Oliver, Annie and sometimes even little Sarah. And, of course, Cyrus planted too. John showed him how. How to harness the mule. How to make the furrows deep and straight. How to hill the plants. Not exactly a garden. Mainly potatoes, and then fields of oats and grass.

Trying to be cheerful. Knowing we were setting an example for the other families. How to work. How to make do. How to show the people in town, the white people, that negroes could work without being beaten. That freedom was a finer master than slavery. And every Sabbath when John held meeting he told our black neighbors, 'As you plant, so shall you reap.' And sometimes they repeated after him, 'As you plant, so shall you reap.'

So the work went on. Day after day. It was never ending. There was no catching up. Work to be done for today. Work to be done for tomorrow. For next week. Next month. Next year. Going to bed tired. All night trying to plan, to arrange the chores, to fit them in, to get them done. And getting up in the morning feeling old and very tired. Too tired to feel anything but old. And sometimes weak. Sometimes with a pain in my back. Sometimes with a pain in my chest. Sometimes with a pain in my belly, feeling as if my belly was heavy, so heavy it would drop from me, like a baby.

Then one day in early summer, flies buzzing, a litter of kittens by the barn, a new calf to be tended, John and Cyrus set fire to the land that was to be burned over and made ready for next year's planting. I was shearing sheep in the corral and I could hear the wild grass sizzle and see the sparks fly up from the tree stumps.

I was almost finished, a heap of good fleece at my side, when I heard Oliver calling, "They're here. They're here."

And at the same time, Sissy, our nearest neighbor came breathless up the hill. "A stampede," she said. "It's a stampede sure enough coming this way."

I put the fleece in a sack, closed the gate and walked to the little knoll. I looked past the fiery land. I looked between the mountains and down the valley. I heard the cattle lowing. I saw their shapes. One against another. A nice sized herd. Moving slowly right through the valley.

"It's the boys," I said to Sissy. "No need to take alarm. It's the boys driving our cattle from Ohio."

Owen hugged me first.

"Took us a few more days than we planned," he said.

"Because we had to stop for a couple of calves," Watson said.

"And the snowmelt in the pass held us up some," Salmon added.

"Lose any heads?" John asked.

"Not a one," Owen said, smiling.

"Whooppee," Frederick said, tossing his hat in the air and catching it on one finger. Annie was clapping her hands. "Whooppee. Whooppee," she said.

"Whooppee. Whooppee," little Sarah said, clapping her hands.

Frederick smiled and swept her up above his head.

"Whooppee," they both said together.

So our family came together again. It was like our house was a flower. A great big flower. No, more like a tree. With roots that could reach past any rocks, with branches that could find the sun.

Was it the last time? Yes, I think it was because soon after that John left for England.

"All our wool is still in the warehouse," he said one evening. "It has to be sold so the growers can get their money. And if I can't sell it here at a fair price, I'll sell it in England."

I stopped spinning.

"But there is so much work to do..." I began.

"I trust you with everything,"' he said. "And the boys are here so there won't be any worry about the hauling and the haying."

Dreams.

Dreaming about Heaven, seeing my children there. Sarah singing in her sweet silvery voice, Charles with a can of worms starting out to fish, Peter and Austin still tumbling over each other like puppies, Amelia smiling like a princess and Ellen, little Ellen just learning to walk. And I was watching. Just standing and watching. And then I was tired and sat down.

"Should I go?" I asked Ruth.

"Maybe it will help you," she said.

"I haven't spoken to your father..."

"But he's not here."

"What do you think he would say?"

"He would say that you have to take care of yourself."

"I would take a room on the third floor, but even so we hardly have the money..."

"Johnny said he would help. And I will stay here and keep everything going."

So I took three woolen blankets, three cotton sheets and pillow cases, six towels, a week's undergarments and a change of clothes and went to Dr. Ruggles' Water Cure Establishment. And it was there one evening that a woman came to speak. And while I listened I thought of Ruth. I thought about girls talking. But it wasn't girls' talk. It was something I had never heard of before. It was what she called woman's talk. It was what she called people's talk.

And soon after that, when John came home from England, he and Oliver joined Johnny, Jase, Owen, Frederick and Salmon in Kansas. "To make it a free state," they said.

CHAPTER 20

HER NAME WAS LUCY STONE.

"No one should be a slave," she said.

Just like that. Simple. Plain. No fancy words.

And, again, "No one should be a slave." she said.

Didn't I know that? Didn't I agree? Didn't I know that my husband was part of this struggle, a leader in the long journey to freedom, and that I was right behind him? Of course, I did. Then why did I feel different, as if I was hearing something new?

Every seat in the main parlor was taken. Men and women sitting in rows, close to each other. Lamps lit against the autumn darkness. The two stoves full and warm. And the tapping of rain on the roof, against the windows.

"Souls are free," she said. "They are born that way and they die that way. And they live that way too—free to grow, to seek the sun, to nourish the fruit which will nourish us all..."

Her voice was silvery, sliding high and then sinking low like a song.

"And this is woman's work," she said. "The work of love and mercy and freedom."

Suddenly a man coughed, stood up, scraped his chair on the floor, stamped his walking stick.

"Sir, what is the matter?" she asked.

He walked to the front of the room.

"Miss Stone," he said. "You are the matter because you are speaking as if you have a right, as if you were a man with a man's right..." And he pointed his walking stick close to her face.

A hush. What would she say—not turning away, facing the man. And facing us. And facing me. Was she looking at me?

"No, sir," she was saying gently but firmly, "I am speaking because I am a woman and because I have a right. I have a God-given right to live and to speak for myself and for others."

A round face with gray eyes, rosy cheeks and an upturned nose. A white collar about her neck. A thin waist. And her voice—still singing, as if she was in church.

"Miss Stone, you are in total and complete error. Misguided at best. And wrong. Absolutely dead wrong," another man said, walking up front to stand next to the first man. "Speaking in public cannot be a God-given right because you are attacking the holy bonds of marriage. You should be at home with a husband and a baby. You should be rocking a cradle and singing a song."

Her voice did not crack. Her eyes did not blink. She was serious—seriously looking at the man, but also looking beyond him. Looking—was she looking at me, in a knowing kind of way, in a neighborly kind of way, nodding—almost smiling?

"No, sir, not at all," she said. "I would never attack marriage as it could be or as it should be because I believe that when a man and a woman are equally free, wedded love can be a pearl which enriches him who gives and him who receives it. And a woman in such a marriage would be glad to rock a cradle and sing a song. And a man in such a marriage would also be free to rock a cradle and sing a song if he had a mind to. Freedom is for everyone. I repeat, freedom is for everyone."

And then a third man.

"Are you saying that our wives and daughters, our sisters and mothers aren't free?" he asked.

And a fourth man.

"What do you know about slavery? What do you know about marriage?" he asked.

What do you know? What do you know? What do you know? Into the hush, like an echo—as if the walls had ears and were listening and then asking...

And the answer.

"But then why have you come to hear me?" she asked. "Or are you here as a common ruffian just to heckle? Nevertheless," she continued when the man did not answer, "if you have a fondness for those questions, I can also ask them. I can ask, Sir, what do you know about slavery?"

"That is a foolish question from a foolish woman," the man answered. "I have ears and eyes."

"And so do I," she said. "And in addition to that, I have a mind and a mouth—and a heart."

She waited a moment. Would the man say something? No, he said nothing.

"So one question has been answered," she said, "but the second question should not be forgotten either. So tell me, Sir, what do you know about a woman's side of marriage?"

A murmur. Was the man saying something? No, the man said nothing. The men nothing. Everyone watching. No one saying anything. The man with the walking stick first, then the second, then the third and fourth man moving out of the way to the side of the room. Standing there.

She continued.

"I know the doom of slavery is everywhere sealed," she said. "And though the warriors are now comparatively few, though alone in the contest, they need not be dismayed, for truth and justice are on their side, and around them, unseen by mortal eyes, are chariots of fire and horsemen of fire, led on by Him who has said that 'the battle is not to the strong.'

"I will tell you a story," she said.

"Once upon a time there was a woman. She had four children. They were all slaves. Even her baby was a slave. But this woman did not want to be a slave and she did not want her children to be slaves. She wanted to escape because just as she had given her children mother's milk, she knew she had to give them freedom. Finally the night came when there was no moon. She woke the older ones first and when they were ready, their meager food in sacks, a sweater tied around their waists, she woke her baby, her little girl. She kissed the child but said nothing, or maybe she whispered, 'We're going to be free.'

And they were free. They were free for three days until they heard the men and dogs behind them. The men and dogs coming closer. So she gathered her children around her. 'Glory to God, we're going to be free,' she shouted. 'We're going to be free.'

And do you know what this woman did? She grabbed her baby and twisted her neck, until her head turned around and she was dead. 'Freedom,' this mother said again, 'if she can not find freedom here, she will find it with the angels...'

"So, ladies and gentlemen, I have told you a story, but it is not a story. For if the warriors in this battle are few, its victims are many."

She looked around the room. She saw the men, one by one returning to their seats. She waited until they sat down. Until the rustling, the moving was done. Until it was quiet. Bone quiet. Even the rain had turned to snow. And looking–yes, she looked at me.

Her lips moved. Was she praying?

I leaned forward to hear her better.

"What is she saying?" the woman next to me asked.

"Freedom," the woman next to her said.

Her voice began to sing again.

"These lines were brought into the world by a woman who knew she was a woman and knew she had a right to speak. Her name is Ada and she is a woman of color.

Then, long as mothers' hearts are breaking
Beneath the hammer of the auctioneer,
And ruthless Avarice tears asunder bonds,
That the fiat of the Almighty joined,
So long should woman's melting voice be heard,
In intercession strong and deep..."

Snowflakes tumbling against the windows. It seemed as if the snow was the only thing moving, that and the tongues of light from the lamps.

"And so it will be, and so it is," Lucy Stone said, "because God reigns supreme and from this discord, this horror, this sin, He will bring peace and harmony. He will bring joy and blessedness. And we must never forget, never lose heart because earth waits long for its harvest time."

The stoves were burning low. It was getting chilly in the

room. I pulled my shawl tighter around my shoulders.

"The time for talking is over," the woman next to me said.

"We talk too much anyway," the woman next to her said.

But they did not stand to leave. I did not stand to leave. No one was standing. No one was leaving.

Finally someone clapped. Then someone else. And then someone else. Soon everyone was clapping. The sound of clapping. The rhythm.

"Clap hands... Clap hands..." the game Sarah had played with Peter and Austin. The game Annie played with little Sarah. I joined them. I clapped my hands together. Freedom. It felt good.

CHAPTER 21

CYRUS HAD A DREAM.

"It was in the night," he began, then hesitated.

"Of course it was in the night," Frederick said. "That's the way dreams come. Did you ever hear of dreams coming in the day?"

"I had a dream too," Watson said, "just the other night when the moon was lollygagging behind a sheet of clouds. I remember the fields were all plowed and it was raining."

"That's the way dreams come because dreams are always there," Frederick continued, "just sitting right there, like on a fence in your head. And sometimes the gate swings shut hard, and the dream falls off and it hurts."

"You can be sure if I had a mind to have a dream, no guessing but it would run itself around cows and hogs," Salmon said, "and then maybe there would be some calves and sheep and..."

"And eggs," Sarah interrupted, "would there be a bonnet of eggs?"

"Oh Sarah," Annie said. "You don't mean bonnet, you mean basket. But the chickens have to come first."

"Cluck. Cluck. Cluck," Annie and Salmon said together and Annie laughed and Sarah laughed too.

Did I smile? I think I did. Maybe it was more of a wonderment than a smile. So little to laugh about. Laughing about chickens and eggs.

It was still light but the sun was quickly slanting low. The boys scraped their plates and Annie stacked them and brought them to the tub. Frederick left the table, went to the door and picked up the axe.

"I'll be splitting some logs," he said. And then as he opened the door, a gust of wind swept into the house like a whirlwind and right along with it Sarah started in to sneeze.

"Close the door, Frederick. Where's your sense? Can't you see the wind picking up?"

And to myself I was saying, 'It's only the dust and dirt of this place that's making her sneeze. Nothing more than that. Nothing more than the dust and the dirt.' The words going through my mind. Saying it over and over. But I set an extra kettle of water to boil, took down the pouch of chamomile leaves and readied the mustard seeds.

"Wait," Oliver called—not shouting, but loud enough so that everyone heard. "Remember Cyrus was going to tell his dream."

Frederick closed the door. Sarah stopped sneezing. Annie took a towel to Sarah's face but Sarah backed up, one step, two, three, walking backwards, almost running until she hit her head against the table.

"Backwards baby goes bump. Backwards baby goes bump," Cyrus was saying softly, almost whispering, stopping when he saw that we were looking at him. That we were waiting. Listening.

He squeezed his hands together and cracked his knuckles.

"My dream? It was in the night," he began again, looking at Frederick. "I mean it was me, it was me who was in the night." And then he stopped, scratched his head, picked at his fingernail. "And it was black," he said more quickly. "The night and me, we were the same, we were both black."

"That's it?" Frederick asked, coming back to the table, sitting down. "That's the dream? That you were black? That the night was black?"

"But you don't understand," Cyrus continued. "Piece by piece, part by part—my foot, my leg, my hand, my arm, my chest, my face—even my face, I could see myself disappearing into the night. And then all that was left was the night."

"Like a ghost?" Watson asked. "Did you become a ghost?"

"No, it wasn't like a ghost. I mean a ghost is something. A ghost can do things. A ghost can see things. But I was nothing.

Just plain nothing. Like the hole in something. Maybe not even the hole."

"Anyway, whoever heard of a black ghost?" Frederick asked. "I never did."

"Because ghosts don't come in black and white," Oliver said, and turning to Cyrus he asked, "Were you afraid?" And when Cyrus didn't answer, he continued, "I would be afraid even if it wasn't the night. I mean if I was trying to find myself and I couldn't. If I was lost..."

Cyrus squeezed his hands together and cracked his knuckles again.

"And then I was hiding," he said.

"It's that law," Frederick began, standing up, grabbing the axe as if he was going to swing it. "But you don't have to worry none because this is our place and we have guns and we have good men. And we know what's right and we aim to do it." He looked at Watson and Salmon and the three of them looked back at Cyrus.

"Where were you hiding?" Annie asked.

"In the night. Just in the night."

"But that's not a real place. Next time you have to hide in the barn."

"Annie, you should know better than that," Salmon said. "Every time you hide in the barn, you get found. The barn is the first place those slave hunters would look."

"Then you could hide in the carriage, behind the seat."

"And that's the second place those people snatchers and catchers would be looking."

"Well, the wheelbarrow is a good place. You could hide in the wheelbarrow and we could cover you with grass and wheel you away."

"I've already done that," Cyrus said. "I've hid in more places than a cottonseed could find."

"Good men," Frederick was saying. "And then there are Matthew and Ben and George. They are all good men, too."

"They are slaves," Cyrus said, "just like me. And just like me they will be hiding or running."

"Or fighting," Frederick insisted. "They could be fighting."

"And how do you think we could do that? How could we fight? Who has the plan? Who has the guns? Who has the shot? Who has the dogs. Who has the whips? Who has the chains? Who has the jails?"

"Who has the right?" Watson asked. "Who has the pain? Who has the sin?"

Quiet.

"It would be better if John were here. He would know what to do. He would know," Cyrus said, cracking his knuckles again.

"Yes, it would be better, but we have ways of knowing too. If there is trouble, we have ways of moving people north. It can be done. It has been done. We have people who will help," I said. "And the Browns are a family, a strong family, and we are not afraid."

Quiet enough to hear the water boiling. And Oliver as he bounced Sarah up and down on his knees.

"I want to ride too," Annie said.

"Okay, two knees for two sisters."

"They're not knees, they're horses," Annie said. "Galloping horses."

"Gidyap," Annie and Sarah said. And they laughed. Yes, they did. They laughed.

I began to steep the tea.

"Cyrus," I said. "You are not a slave here. No one is a slave here. That's the way it is, and that's the way it will be."

Then, as if we were being tested, there was a knock on the door. We looked at each other. Cyrus moved toward the back room. Frederick raised his axe, Salmon standing on one side of him, Watson on the other. And then we heard that it was Matthew's knock, three little ones, one loud one, two soft ones.

"It's just Matthew," Annie said, running to the door, opening it.

"Now just tell me what you folks are doing huddled in this house when there's still a little light left to do some ploughing if we hurry?"

Mathew's voice boomed as he came into the house, his wife Matilda behind him. Young and slender, sometimes they looked as if they were prancing instead of walking, like a pair of matched horses. I could see them hitched to the surrey, taking the white family to church.

Sarah ran to Matilda. Matilda caught her, scooped her up and turned her around.

"Watch that you don't dizzy her," Matthew said.

And then another knock, even though the door was open.

"It's me," Winifred said. She was carrying the cloth I needed to make shoes, carrying it in her arms like she was carrying a baby.

"Ben is sick," she said, putting the sack down. "A bad cough and maybe a fever. He's just been doing poorly ever since he was stuck deep in that snowdrift last month." She shivered. "It's so cold. It's always so cold."

"Timbucto is not Alabama, no mistaking that..." Matilda began.

"And that's a blessing if there ever was one," Matthew interrupted. "So don't forget to be mindful of it and to thank the good Lord every day. And while we are into thanking don't forget there's God's right hand helper on this earth, Mr. Gerritt Smith who gave us this land and then there are these people, right here, these white people, who helped us out like we were kin."

"Of course, of course," Winifred said, looking around the room, trying to smile. "I know that, of course. Didn't Mary midwife my little Angelina..."

I put my arm around her shoulders. She was cold.

"Just a few minutes and we'll take some chamomile tea down to Ben," I said, "but first you should have something for your bones and your blood."

I filled a bowl with hot chicken broth.

"Sit down and eat it while it's hot but don't gulp it down."

"Yes, ma'am," she said.

"Winifred, you know you don't have to ma'am me."

"Yes, ma'am," she said.

Talking like a little girl, the way my girls said ma'am and sir. Talking like that when she should have been talking like a grown up person. It was one of the things that slavery did—keep you like a little girl forever. And another thing that slavery did was twist words. It said black, black, black when anyone could see, when anyone would say that Winifred was white. Almost white. A misty white. And she had blue eyes.

A woman of color, Winifred sometimes said, and that sounded good. A woman of color could be a pink tone, or a blue tint, or a hint of yellow or orange, or a trace of brown. She could be a woman of her own color, not black or white. But that's not the way it was. The way it was made Winifred seem poor, as if she came from no one, as if she was a motherless, fatherless child. With no roots. No family. Just sprung up out of herself. And then I started to think about Ruth's Eva and the bonnet that matched their blue eyes. And then I was thinking about more than Eva. Well, maybe not thinking about more, but thinking behind her or past her. Thinking about black and white. And if I was black would I be saying, 'Yes ma'am, no ma'am' to any woman who was white? Saying it and not even thinking what I was saying. But I would care. Yes, deep down, I would care.

I shook my head. I wanted to say that maybe the problem was in our heads, in our eyes and not in our skin. I mean if we didn't see color, it would be so simple. So glorious. But I didn't say that. I didn't say anything. I wasn't afraid but it just didn't happen. No matter, I said to myself. Saying isn't as important as doing and saying isn't as important as believing.

The boys left with Matthew and Matilda.

Annie took Sarah out to the barn.

Cyrus went to tend to the new lamb. "And John?" he asked as he left, "do you know when he will be returning?"

"Soon," I said. "Maybe next week."

Winifred finished the soup and scrubbed the table. I scrubbed the pots and pans.

"Sissy's with the baby for a spell, so there's no need to hurry back, is there, ma'am?" she asked.

"No, no need to hurry if Ben doesn't need us. And thank you for the shoe cloth," I said, putting it in my work box.

"It's Ben who got it for doing some carpenter's work in town. If he's not ailing he scoots after work more than anyone. He wants us to be a family. He wants us to have things. And he's good with his hands." She stopped. "Did Mr. John make that cradle?" she asked.

"No," I began, looking at the cradle, thinking back. "Well now that you ask," I continued, "I don't absolutely know that because the cradle has always been there. I mean it was there when I became Mrs. Brown."

I looked at the cradle. I opened my eyes and looked at it like it was the first time I was seeing it. The worn out parts. The cracks. So many babies had been in that cradle. So many...

I closed my eyes but I couldn't see them. Well, maybe I could see one or two. My first baby, my first Sarah, I saw her, and I heard her, talking to herself, trying to catch a shadow or a dancing sunlight spot.

But why was the cradle still there, in plain view? Why wasn't it tucked away in the bedroom or the barn? Why didn't I give it to Winifred when she had her baby?

"I haven't had babies for a while. Sarah is four," I began. "And she's my second Sarah..."

"I lost a baby too," Winifred said.

"But Sarah wasn't a baby when she was taken. She was my first born. She was my big girl. She was the best berry finder we had and she was just learning to seat a horse and she liked to sing psalms and teach the little ones."

"Got scorched in the sun. It was my baby but it wasn't Ben's."

"God works in mysterious ways," I said. "I had a baby that got burned too."

We looked at each other. Not really blue, thicker than that, her eyes were gray, the color of the sky before a storm.

I took out my yarn.

"Just dyed this," I said, looping it over the back of a chair. "It's for Ruth's baby."

"Pink and blue. It's pretty, ma'am," she said, touching it lightly. "In the big house, all the babies had blankets like that."

I smiled. Was it the first time I wasn't worrying about being too frivolous or too fancy? I think so.

"And it's likely I'll trim it with colored bows," I added.

Winifred cleared her throat.

"Ben wants to go, ma'am," she said. "He wants to go to

Canada. It's too hard here and it's too cold."

I started to wind the blue yarn into balls.

"Do you think Canada is a sunny place?" I asked.

"I don't know about sunny, but we won't be settling in the wilderness—Ben promised. And I won't have to fall down on the ice to milk the cows. And maybe the wind won't howl through the walls. And maybe there will be a town we can walk to. A store. A church. A meeting place. It's so hard here. Like the ground itself. Cold, hard and dark—and lonely."

Yarn slipped off my lap. She bent to pick it up.

"Everyone wants to go, ma'am," she continued, "except maybe Matthew and Matilda. And Cyrus—he'll stay here as long as you do."

I wasn't surprised. Didn't I also think about going? How many times? More times than I could remember. Not that I told anyone. Not even Ruth.

"Home is where your heart is. Home is where your husband is," she would have said.

And I would agree, but your heart isn't like a stone just plopped down in one place. Your heart could also be in different places, and if it was, it was,—there was nothing much you could do about it.

"But it's not right," John said, when he came home. He was shaking his finger at Ben. "You're running away. Good never comes from running away."

"We're not cowards, if that's what you mean," Ben said.

"You're fooling yourselves. Even worse, you're betraying yourselves..."

"We're going to Canada. You're going to Ohio. What's the difference?"

"The difference is I'm not giving up. I'm still in the fight. And after we sell the sheep and buy supplies, we'll be back."

Ben turned away. The others did too.

"Running away," John said to me, waving his hands as if he was waving our neighbors gone. "Just pulling up roots and running away when they should be digging in. Tut, tut, tut... What did they learn while they were here? Have we failed them?"

"They learned to live without masters and they learned to go without masters," I said, turning with John to the house. "And isn't that what we wanted?"

It was fall, the time of harvest and haying, but after the chores, the next week, half of our neighbors were ready to leave. John gave them a wagon and with what they had, they made a little caravan, Ben leading the way.

"To Canada," he said. "To freedom."

"Amen," they said.

"Good luck," Matthew said.

"Take good care of that baby Angelina," Matilda said.

"And don't freeze," Sissy said.

"I'll try not to," Winifred smiled.

Then I gave Winifred the pink and blue blanket.

"But it's for Ruth..." she began.

"I've already finished half of another one," I said. "And besides, I owe you and Ben for the shoe cloth."

Angelina started to cry.

Ben held the reins ready. "Cyrus," he called out, "last chance, you can still come along."

Cyrus shook his head.

Ben lifted the reins, let them fall. The caravan started to move.

It was like the earth was turning into itself and also away from itself. The way we had all come together, the way most of us were leaving. Cyrus, too, not going to Canada, but going his own way, even though John said he should come with us.

"Ohio is a free state and we can fight that vile and vicious law. I swear to you with the Lord's help, we can beat it," John said. "But you can't beat it if you don't fight it. And if you don't fight it, you're a slave. You'll always be a slave."

"I don't care about fighting," Cyrus said. "I'm going to load my horse and go west. And when I get to California I'm going to prospect for gold. Do you know what I want?" he asked John.

John shook his head.

"I want to become rich. I want to burn candles all night long. I don't even want to know what the night looks like. If you have money you can catch the night by its tail and turn it right smart around."

So Cyrus left Timbucto, but before he did, he helped John fix the carriage wheel and put up the fence around Ellen's grave.

This time I did not cry. I kissed the little stone. Just plain. No carving on it. No time to do any carving. Annie and Sarah brought flowers. Ruth came with a tray of dough cakes filled with jelly. We said a prayer. We sang a hymn—the music staying in my mind all the way back to Ohio.

And how long did we stay in Ohio? In Mr. Perkins' house in Akron? In the house where Amelia was born, where she died. In the house where Sarah, little Sarah was born. How long is long? Long enough to have another baby, a boy. Kicking and crying, he seemed so big and strong, but two weeks later he was dead. Two weeks later I was sick with bleeding lungs.

And then a year later, another baby. A girl.

"Ellen," I said.

"Ellen," John agreed.

CHAPTER 22

MEN TRAVEL. IT SEEMS THEY ARE CALLED into the world with a horn or a drum and they hear it and march with it. Marching away. Riding away. One way or another, they follow the call to go. East or west. North or south. Summer or winter.

And the letters begin.

"I've sold the farm and I'm moving to Kansas," Johnny wrote. "We are needed to defend the Negro against the proslavery scoundrels who would fasten slavery on that glorious land by any means, fair or foul."

Jase agreed.

"I'm moving with Johnny," he wrote. "It's what has to be done, and no matter what, we'll do what has to be done to make Kansas a free state. And," he added," I'm taking the best of my newly grafted grapevines and fruit trees."

A few days later there were letters from Owen and Frederick.

"Johnny and Jase have their families to move," Owen wrote, "so Frederick and I will drive the horses and cattle."

"We'll be in Kansas when the grass turns green," Frederick wrote, "ready to settle and ready to vote. And when the votes are counted, Kansas will be as free as a bird."

Men traveling. They hear something. They see something. They know something and they go. Taking their families with them sometimes. Their women and their children. Taking their babies—and sometimes having to leave them, like Jase and his baby—how he left his baby on the side of the trail, his tiny grave marked by a peach tree.

And then Salmon.

"Salmon, too?" I asked. "Salmon is going?"

"They need him," John said.

And Salmon stood up, so tall and straight and strong. I shook my head. I knew I wasn't supposed to be seeing the baby in him. I knew I was supposed to be seeing the man.

"Driving the herd and wintering them won't be easy," John continued, "what with Frederick's headaches and Owen's bad arm. Salmon will be a big help."

"Of course," I said, "of course," because it would make no more sense to try to keep him home than to try to keep the wind from blowing. Because to keep him home would be narrow and selfish and sinful. Because they were making a life in Kansas. A new life for themselves. A free life for the slaves.

And then a few months later, after we moved back to the northland, Johnny wrote again. "We've plowed ten acres for corn and another acre for a garden in which we planted everything and anything we could—onions, cabbages, peas, squash, garden beans, lettuce, cucumbers, water and musk melons, early turnips and potatoes."

"This is it," John said as he sat to answer the letter. "Settling in Kansas is the beginning. The real beginning. The chance to turn the tide. The chance to make the Lord's will manifest. The chance to prove ourselves equal to the challenge."

He looked at me. I don't know what he saw. An old woman? A tired old woman? A tired old woman clutching her baby?

I looked at John. How many years had we been married? Twenty-two years? Yes, almost exactly that. So long ago I hardly remembered what he looked like then. Now his hair was backing off his forehead and mostly gray. His shoulders were a little more rounded. But his muscles were strong and his hands were still large. They were open on the table as he looked at me. I knew those hands. Those hands knew me. Those hands had known me.

And then another letter from Johnny. A different letter.

"We need money. We need guns. We have among the five of us, 1 Revolver, 1 Bowie Knife, 1 middling good Rifle, 1 poor Rifle, 1 small pocket pistol and 2 sling shot. You can imagine that we are woefully underarmed. For each of us we need 1 Colts large sized Revolver, 1 "Allen & Thurbers" large size Revolver, 1 Minnie Rifle and 1 heavy Bowie Knife. And we need men," he wrote. "Now is the time. There is no turning back. The hour is striking."

"The hour is striking," John repeated, reading the letter over and over again. "The hour is indeed striking. And if it is so painful for us to part with the hope of meeting again, how of the poor slaves?"

So John left. He went to Rochester. He went to Springfield. He went to Syracuse. He went to Akron. He wrote, "I expect to leave here today and shall probably be on my way to Cleveland tomorrow. I have met with such good encouragement from the people here in the way of contributions in guns, revolvers, swords, powder caps and money that I thought it best to detain a day or two longer."

In Cleveland John met Oliver and they went in a one-horse wagon, sometimes only going six or eight miles a day. John wrote, "Our load is heavy so that we have to walk most of the time." Six weeks later joining Johnny, Jase, Owen, Frederick and Salmon in Kansas. In Osawatomie, Kansas. And Ruth's husband, Henry, went too. It was the year after the drought, 1855, and all our menfolk were in Kansas. Watson was the only one to stay in Timbucto.

"You'll be helping the cause in a different way," John had told him. "There's more than one way to skin a cat and there's more than one cat to be skinned."

I watched. Watching. Watching. Thinking that so much of my life was disappearing. Slowly. Seeing John mount his horse, turning its head, starting at a slow easy pace. Watching until he was gone and Ellen started crying and Watson finished the milking and Annie was taking bread out of the oven and Sarah had set the table and Ruth was stirring the stew and feeding her baby.

"Let them go," Ruth said. "The Lord is not blind. He will watch over them and over us too. And we know that we can't look back to what was. We have to look forward to what will be."

She took John's Old Testament from the shelf and opened it.

"As the sun rose upon the earth and Lot entered Zoar," she read, "the Lord rained upon Sodom and Gomorrah sulfurous fire from the Lord out of heaven. He annihilated those cities and the entire Plain, and all the inhabitants of the cities and the vegetation of the ground. And Lot's wife looked back and she thereupon turned into a pillar of salt.

"So don't look back. Don't ever look back," Ruth said again, closing the book.

But memories? Are they backwards, looking back? And how do you leave a memory?

"Most of the time I don't look back," I said, thinking that if I looked back, how could I plant a garden? How could I hem or stitch trousers? How could I look for those little yellow birds, the way they hop and sing? How could I hold Ellen so tight to me?

"And I'm not saying it's for me to know," I continued, "but maybe Lot's wife just wanted to remember, maybe she was looking back so she could remember, so she could say goodbye. Maybe it was the only way she could go forward."

Ruth didn't answer. I don't think she did. She just put the Bible back on the shelf, covered the stewpot and started to mix a paste to chink in a hole in the front wall.

So there we were in Timbucto, in the town of North Elba, in the arms of the Adirondack Mountains, in a house that Ruth's husband had built for us. A small house, but big enough for the small family we had become–just Watson, Annie and Sarah and Ellen. And then Ruth and her baby came.

"The men are together and we should be together too," she said.

And then when Ruth's brother-in-law went to Kansas, his wife came. And when Watson married, his wife came. And I was feeling better. My lungs had stopped bleeding. My hands and feet had stopped swelling. My stomach was more settled. My strength was returning. And Ellen, my little Ellen, was stronger too.

I sorted the wool I had and readied the spinning wheel and

loom. I pulled the iron kettle next to the door to use for hog butchering and rendering. I baked. I pickled. I canned. When we could we went looking for apples and nuts and berries. Sarah was like her namesake when it came to berry picking. She could get those berries that were low on the ground or hard to reach and she was always on the lookout for snakes.

Summer giving way to the darkness of winter. The long shadow of winter. The wind whistling through the house. I wove three new blankets that winter and made Annie a good heavy coat. But the shoes had to wait for the spring.

And I stopped watching, stopped looking past the field and the houses. Stopped looking down the road and into the distance. Hardly noticing that one day flowed into the next, but as soon as I could I hung a side of meat. I rolled bandages to send to Kansas. And I waited for the letters to come.

"I am sending you a barrel of good flour," John wrote.

"Dig the potatoes sparingly and do not waste the hay," he wrote.

"Ellen is complaining a little with worms," I answered. "And Ruth's baby is dreadful cross."

"Salmon almost died of bilious colic," he wrote, "and Johnny, Jase and his wife Ellen, Owen and Frederick are all sick with the ague."

"Snow is not all gone in the fields," I wrote. "There is plenty to be seen on the mountains. The beech and maple trees look almost as dry as they did in January, hardly a bud to be seen on them yet."

"We are doing the Lord's work, but do not think that we are in Paradise," he wrote.

"I am trying to keep out of debt," I answered. "We have made 64 pounds of sugar, about 3 gallons of molasses and a little vinegar. It was a very poor year for making sugar. Last week we were on our last loaf and I didn't know what to do. Watson decided to write to Father Brown for help."

And Oliver was so lonesome he wrote to Watson, "I've written to you, now you must spur up about writing, and Annie too."

And Wealthy, Johnny's wife, wrote, "Our men have so

much war and elections to attend to that it seems as though we were a great while getting into a house."

"But our reunion may be sooner than we think," John wrote. "Indeed, I believe Missouri is fast becoming discouraged about making Kansas a slave state, and I think the prospect of its becoming free is brightening every day. Try to be cheerful, and always hope in God, who will not leave nor forsake them that trust Him."

And then the other news. The news that didn't come in a letter. The news that someone told someone and someone told Ruth.

"There was a slaughter," she said quietly, clasping her hands tightly together. "A slaughter..."

"A slaughter? Hogs?" I asked, knowing it wasn't that, knowing I was asking just to be saying something, just to be saying something that was around something else.

"A slaughter," Ruth said again, just as quietly.

A slaughter. A killing of people. A killing of people in the middle of the night. A rounding up of people. A killing of people in their dooryards. Taken from their beds and into their dooryards and killed there. With swords and guns. Blood flowing into the night. Into the darkness.

"And the men?" I asked.

"The men who were killed were proslavery settlers. And the men who did the killing—they said it was John Brown and his sons."

I closed my eyes. No, my eyes were so heavy, they closed by themselves. And I shivered. In the middle of May, I shivered. "Could it be? How could it be?" I mumbled. I took Ruth's hand. "How could it be?" I asked. "My husband? My sons?"

"We don't know," she said. "We don't know anything. We're not sure. It was just one report in one paper. Maybe it wasn't. Maybe it was someone else or something else."

But I thought I saw tears in her eyes and she bowed her head. "The Lord is my shepherd," she began, "I shall not want..."

"I don't believe it," Watson said. "It's a trick. It's a dirty trick. It's a lie."

"It's a trick. It's lie," Annie agreed. "I know it's a lie. Father wouldn't do that. He would fight but he wouldn't just kill somebody. Remember when he said, 'Vengeance is mine saith the Lord. I shall repay'?"

"But didn't he also say an eye for an eye and a tooth for a tooth?" Ruth was whispering.

Sarah slapped her hands against the table. "Father wouldn't take anybody's eye," she said, "and he wouldn't take anybody's tooth."

Ellen started to cry.

"She always cries," Sarah said.

"That's because she's a baby," Annie said, picking her up. She brought her to the table. She soaked a piece of bread in milk and gave it to her.

"Ruth is right," I said. "We don't know. And if we don't know, we have to wait. We have to wait until we do know. Doesn't that make sense? And we have to believe." I did not say we should be cheerful. How could we be cheerful?

No one was crying. Just breathing. And that's the way it was, just breathing one day into the next. No crying. No questions. No answers. Praying every morning and praying every night. And breathing. Blowing the days together and past each other into weeks.

Into letters. Into answers.

"We encountered quite a number of pro-slavery men," John wrote, "and took quite a number of prisoners. Our prisoners we let go, but we kept some four or five horses. After this we were accused of murdering five men at Pottawatomie, and great efforts have since been made by the Missourians and their ruffian allies to capture us."

Ruth smiled as I read the letter.

"At last we know," she said. "Father didn't do it."

She hugged her sisters-in-law. Three women just standing in the middle of the kitchen hugging each other. And then the circle widened, and I hugged too.

"See," Watson said. "I told you it was a lie."

And the next letter.

"Henry was shot in the lungs but he is recovering quickly.

Salmon was badly kicked by a horse and needs much rest. Owen too, who is suffering from a long lasting fever. And Frederick's wild headaches have returned."

And the next letter.

"We are in hiding, dwelling like David of Old, with the serpents of the rocks and the wild beasts of the wilderness."

Hunted. My husband. My sons. Hunted like animals. Hunted like slaves. But what could we do? What could I do? That was in Kansas—so far away, it could have been another country. In Heaven or Hell. And for us in North Elba the days came and went as they always did. The grass was growing. Old Spot was giving a nice mess of milk. Watson gave the Hinkleys a calf and got two little pigs in return. And he sowed about four acres of rye and some carrots and turnips.

And then Salmon came home.

The chickens squawked and I heard a tumbling. And when I opened the door there were Watson and Salmon slapping each other on the back.

"Pottawatomie," Salmon said after dinner. "That's where it happened." He shook his head. He drew his eyebrows tight together. "But maybe it had to be done."

"What?" I asked. "What had to be done?"

"They burned Lawrence. They took prisoners. It was a time to fight fire with fire."

"Answer my question. What had to be done?"

"We knew who was who and we knew who did what. And Charles Sumner was almost beaten to death when he was in the Senate chamber."

"The men in Pottawatomie beat Charles Sumner?"

"Of course, not the same men. But they're all the same, all low on the goose, pro-slavery men. And father said we had to show that there were two sides to this thing."

"Father? What did father do?"

Quiet. The sound of spring peepers rising from the creek. A whippoorwill. And that—a mourning dove?

What was Salmon saying? What was it that Salmon was not saying? What had John done?

"And then what happened?" Watson asked, putting down

the wheel he was fixing.

"The Buford Company came in from Missouri and burned everything. Every house in Brown's Station. When they got through, there was no more Brown's Station. And Johnny's house, with all his books, burned the longest. And then they found Johnny and arrested him."

"And Henry?" Ruth asked. "What about Henry?"

"Henry is safe. He wasn't caught. Johnny and Jase were the only two they found and arrested. And Johnny was beaten. He was chained and beaten. He was screaming and crying, twisting and turning. Kicking. Jase said Johnny was like a crazy man."

Johnny? My Johnny? How could that be? I never saw him crazy. I always saw him careful, looking to the up and down of anything before he would say yes or no.

"And Jase was shouting to save Johnny, 'Don't kill him. He's sick. Don't kill him. He's crazy.' But they put Jase on a horse, tied his arms behind his back and almost lynched him."

"And then what happened?" Watson asked, anger climbing into his voice.

"They were pulled off their horses and driven like that, in their chains. And when they stumbled and fell, they were dragged up and driven again. 'You like Negroes so much, you should like being slaves,' one of the soldiers shouted and the others laughed, dragging them up and driving them faster. From the prison in Osawatomie to the prison in Lecompton. Sixty-five miles they were driven like that, dragging their chains after them. And when they got to Lecompton, Jase went before a magistrate. "I never knowingly injured any man," he said. And the magistrate was honest enough to believe him and had him released.

"Then Jase asked, 'What about my brother? He was not at Pottawatomie. And he is not a murderer.'"

The magistrate turned to Johnny. "What is your name?" he asked.

"I am a lamb," he answered.

"Who are you?" the magistrate asked again.

"I used to be a shepherd, now I am the flock," he answered, running his hands through his hair and then holding them outstretched as if he was blessing something or someone.

I stood up. Moved toward the door. Saw the fields. The mountains. God's work as John liked to say. God's work and man's work together. That's the way it was supposed to be. But it was hard. So hard. I closed my eyes but a tear ran down my face. Then two. Then three. My honorable Johnny. My kind and gentle Jase. And what of Frederick? And Oliver—so young? And Salmon, who said it needed to be done? And again I was thinking of Dianthe. Seeing her getting larger, than smaller. Did angels come in different sizes? Was my first little Ellen as big as my first Sarah? And Charles? And Peter? And Austin? And Amelia? But I couldn't see. There was fog between us. There was smoke.

And that was the talking we did, the only talking we did about Pottawatomie, about what happened there. I suppose some things are best not known. Let sleeping dogs lie, they say. And what was done was done. Blood couldn't be put back into corpses. They couldn't be stood up and sent back to their houses, to their families. It was not a time to look back. This had to be the time to look forward. To think of the time when the slaves would be free. And maybe when that happened, we would also be freed—a little, freed of burden, freed of responsibility.

Once again the summer ended quickly, too quickly. Almost suddenly. Aspens turning yellow and dropping their leaves. The maples turning red. Flaming red. Their leaves holding on as long as they could.

Salmon and Watson were digging potatoes on one of those clear, cool days when Ruth came running her horse up the road.

"Frederick's been shot," she said, as soon as she was close enough to be heard. "Frederick?" Salmon asked.

Ruth nodded. "Isabella got the news in town."

"But he was innocent. He was there but he didn't do anything." Salmon said. "He ran a snarling dog through, that's all that he did. He killed a dog, that's all. Then he turned away from anything else."

So there it was. As plain as anything could be plain. There had been killing and John had lied. There had been killing and Salmon was there. How many of my sons were there with their father? And Frederick—poor Frederick, always trying so hard to be strong, to be strong enough to please John...

"He just walked out of the house around to the back to feed the horses and he was shot. Just like that," Ruth said.

"But he was innocent," Salmon said again. "And when Jase asked him if he had killed anyone, he was crying and he said he couldn't do it."

Salmon dropped his shovel. Then Watson dropped his shovel. They left their big rush baskets half filled with tubers, and made ready to go to Kansas. To find their brother's killer and to kill him.

I was not a man. I was not in Kansas. I was not fighting. I did not feel as if I was dying. I did not feel as if I was living or dying. I felt as if I was a mountain, children rolling from me like stones down a mountainside. Well, that was one part, the part of feeling strong, of putting a shoulder to the storm, of turning your back, your face to it and then standing up when the storm is past. But the other part was doors. I dreamt of doors. Not being able to open or close them. All kinds of doors—big and small, rough and smooth, front and back.

"Leave the door open," I would tell anyone who came or went—or else I would be trapped.

Why? Did someone say it was forbidden? Did someone say, Mary Brown, you can be a wife and mother, but you can't be a doorkeeper? That you must come to doors as you find them, leave them as you found them? That you can have a house but can't own it? That you can live in a house but can't lock it?

Did someone say to be careful? That it is easy to be trapped and hard to be free? That I must learn? That I must accept? That I must believe?

It was a dream of more than one night. And I knew it was a dream of coming and going. And I knew it made no difference if the door was open or closed. The coming and going would go on. It had to go on. Once it started, it wouldn't stop. It couldn't.

And John? Some people were calling him Captain Brown or Osawatomie Brown. They said he was a champion, a commander, a leader. They said he was fiery, strong. as steel, and straight as an arrow. The newspapers called him the terror of Missouri. Owen said he was the most daring, courageous man in Kansas.

I was not surprised. And if I was worried, I was also satisfied. He was doing what had been given to him. He was opening doors. He was leading the way.

But as time went on, it was also true that John Brown, the one who was defending the town of Lawrence, the one who was helping slaves to escape, the one who was on guard against the Border Ruffians, the one who drilled his men to be soldiers, the one who made my sons soldiers–doing what soldiers do, sometimes that John Brown felt as if it was just a name. A name that also rolled down and away from me, like a stone.

CHAPTER 23

HER NAME WAS ARAMINTA ROSS.

She stood in a doorway. She faced a man. A white man. She blocked the doorway. The man was an overseer. He couldn't chase a slave. He couldn't catch the slave who was running away. She was in the way. She put herself in the way. Freedom... she was held by its sound, by the slave escaping. She was held a minute, two minutes, until she was hit in the head with a two pound weight. Then she fell like a stone. Blood spilled from a deep gash in her forehead.

She was betwixt and between, not in this world and not in the next. She was in her cabin in the slave quarter, but she was beyond it.

"Minty is sure enough facing the other world," one slave said.

"She's soon to die," another said.

"And who are you?" Araminta's mother asked angrily. "Are you the Lord? Are you the Lord's messenger to know who is coming and going? And yesterday she opened an eye. And today she sucked in some soup and gravy. And this morning she was praying. Lord was she praying. So hard. So long. Praying for the master's soul. Praying for the master's heart–to change it."

"She was too uppity," a third slave said. "She put a rag on her head and thought she was a lady."

"The likes of her makes it worse than bad for the rest of us. Better she should have been knocked out of the way. Better she should have been whipped."

"Whipped?" Araminta's mother turned from her daughter lying on a sheet on the floor. How many months? From the time the corn was husked, through Christmas, through the whole winter, till now—almost seeding time.

"I'll tell you about whipping," her mother continued. "At her first hiring out, but six years old, she was whipped. At her second hiring out to that poor white Cook family, she ran away and hid in a pig sty. For a week she fought with the pigs for the potato peelings and the apple cores. And then when she went back to that house, she got enough whipping scars for an old field hand. Scars were strung across her neck like wire. See them there. See them here and there."

"It's the truth that scars can turn your head, anybody's head, 'specially a young girl's head."

"Mark my words, say goodbye to Minty. Her hiring out days are over. The master will sell her, sure enough."

Araminta's mother was quiet. She had already lost two daughters, taken away in chains. She could still feel their bodies shaking, see the tears streaming down their faces—and then hear the clank of the chains.

She had run to the overseer. She had run to the master. "Please don't do this to old Rit," she said. "Please don't do this to faithful Simon..."

But it was done. As quick as a cloud moving to cover the sun. The coffle was a blur. The chains were a murmur. And the singing drifted back like the tidewater returning to shore.

I'll send you my love by the whip-o'will;
The dove shall bring my sorrow;
I leave you a drop of my heart's own blood,
For I won't be back tomorrow...

Araminta was working in the fields then, but she heard. Everyone heard. Everyone shook. Fear. That was it. Fear of the unknown, because there was no news after going south. No word. No sign. No nothing. Like going over the edge of the world.

It was the spring of 1835 on a plantation in Maryland. Araminta was fifteen years old. Slowly she was recovering from the hole in her head. Slowly the blood stopped spilling. Slowly the skin started to come together. Slowly the pus and the blood hardened. Slowly a scar marked her forehead.

And slowly she was getting stronger. Eating. Sleeping. Looking when her mother opened the door to let someone in. Saying hello. Saying goodbye. Looking when the door was pushed open. Looking at the men. The master. The overseer. The farmers the overseer brought to see her, to buy her. But she had stood in a doorway. She had refused to move. Who would buy her? And although she had been strong, she still wasn't well, falling into a deep sleep for no reason, at any time.

They shook their heads. They laughed. "She's not worth a sixpence," one farmer after the other said.

So Araminta prayed. She could be taken away. Everything could be taken away. Only God—only God could be hers, in her head, in her heart, on her lips—the breath of life. "Please, Lord, don't let me be sold. Turn that man around so Jesus can find him. So Jesus can lift the meanness from that man's heart."

And then the slave trader, Mr. Woodfolk, came. Did he look at her? Maybe once.

"Put her in the lot," he said.

She was young, she would be strong again—and a woman could never be as much trouble as a man.

"Harriet Ross," the overseer said. "Her Christian name is Harriet."

"Make out the papers," Mr. Woodfolk said.

Sold.

And then her energy turned into hating. Or maybe not hating, but just wanting to be free. Maybe not even that—because what did she know of freedom?

Sold.

The word pounded into her head, as if she was already chained. And she prayed, "Lord, if you're not going to change that man's heart, then kill him and take him out of the way. Then kill him and take him out of the way," she repeated.

Sold.

If that happened, she might fall asleep on that long trip. She wouldn't know where she was or what she was doing. She wouldn't be able to move. She would be beaten. She would die there on that road. Alone on that road. In chains.

Praying. She prayed to the Lord. She listened for the Lord's answer.

Was it the Lord's answer when the doctor came? And then the news from the bedroom to the kitchen to the stable to the quarter where the little children heard, telling the field hands when they brought them water. And then a song breaking into the silence, slowly...

He know moon-rise, he know star-rise
But he done lain his body down.

Old master'll walk in the moonlight, he'll walk in the starlight
To lay his body down.

Old master'll lie in the grave and stretch out his arms,
To lay his body down.

The master was dead.

Anxious eyes from one slave to another. Would there be a selling of slaves? Who would be sold? When? Where?

The new master came. He talked to the overseer.

"You will not be sold," the overseer said.

And they returned to the fields, to the forests, to the Big House, to their cabins. They returned to their lives, grateful for having what they had.

"Glory be to God, who looks after His children," Harriet prayed. "But," she added, "if there is sin big or small in my heart wipe it away. For Jesus' sake sweep the sin from my heart."

Days passing into weeks and Harriet felt better. Soon she was well enough to be hired out to Mr. Stewart. And strong enough.

"I can do a man's job," she said.

"I'll let you try," Mr. Stewart agreed.

So she lifted barrels. She plowed fields. She loaded wagons. She drove an oxcart. She split logs. She shouldered timbers. She swung a broadax and cut a half cord of wood a day.

And Harriet learned about the forest. How to live in the forest. How to find her way through the forest. Quietly.

"Hat, you walk like an Injun," her father said. "A leaf doesn't rustle and a twig doesn't crack when you come through here."

Walking through the forest, learning how to look toward the sky and find the North Star, the freedom star.

Sometimes remembering this hymn, humming it:

And what shall be my journey,
How long I'll stay below,
Or what shall be my trials,
Are not for me to know.

In every day of trouble
I'll raise my thought on high,
I'll think of that bright temple
And crowns above the sky.

Then Harriet married. Of course, she wanted her life with her husband to be long and sweet and soft, but sometimes she felt strange. She wondered why a free man would want to marry a slave.

"There's nobody says that I'm marrying a slave," he said. "I'm marrying the girl, plain and simple."

So Harriet became the wife of John Tubman. She lived with him. She loved him. But she was still a slave and she still worked for the Master, where he said she should work, what he said she should do. And she could be sold.

"John," Harriet said, when there were whispers that the slave traders were coming, "we have to run away. We have to go north."

"If you go north, you'll freeze," John said. "You'll die just as surely as if you go south. North or south no one ever came back from either place."

"But I would be free," Harriet said.

"You would be dead," her husband answered. "How free is that?"

She felt a headache coming on. She lowered her voice.

"I have dreams," she said. "I can see the slave traders coming. I can see the slaves chained together. I can hear the women screaming. I am screaming..."

"There's no sense to that," John said. "It's because of your scar. That's the whole story of it."

"And I have another dream," Harriet continued. "I dream that I am flying, flying over everything, the fields, the rivers, the mountains. And then when it seems my strength is giving out and I am sinking down, there are ladies all dressed in white and they help me. They hold me and pull me across."

"And who are those ladies? And how are you going to get there?"

"There's the star," Harriet began, "it twinkles.."

"How will you travel when the night is cloudy?" he asked. "How will you know where you are? How will you read a sign? How will you read a note? And what will happen if you fall asleep just when slave hunters are near? And what will you eat? And where will you stay?"

"The Lord tells me I have a right," Harriet said slowly. "I have a right to two things—freedom or death."

"You have a right to nothing," John said. "And if you keep on being crazy, if your feet start listening to your head, I'll tell the Master right away. You're not a hound dog and you're not a Moses."

Harriet looked at her husband. "I have a right..." she said again.

A woman alone. Following a dream. Following a star. Traveling. Talking to the Lord. Listening to the Lord. Was she crazy?

Through forests, over rugged mountain passes, hiding in potato holes, finding the stations on the underground railroad, wading across the rivers. Feeling safe. Explaining. "Just so long as the Lord wants to use me, He will take care of me, and when He doesn't want me any longer, I am ready to go." Saying, "I always tell the Lord, 'I'm going to hold steady onto you, and you've got to see me through.'"

Talking to the Lord. Praying. Hearing the Lord—stop, leave

the road, turn away from the danger ahead—the posters promising a reward, the slave catchers waiting.

Carrying a pistol. Holding a pistol to a man's head. "Dead niggers tell no tales. You go on or die," she said. Giving the babies paregoric, carrying them in a basket.

Escaping. How many times? How many people? Three hundred people. Back and forth, back and forth, from slavery to freedom, from Maryland to Philadelphia, from Maryland to Canada. She led three hundred people from Egypt's land to freedom, to live under the lion's paw. They sang:

You may hinder me here, but you can't up there,
Let my people go.
He sits in the heavens and answers prayer,
Let my people go.

Oh go down, Moses,
Way down into Egypt's land,
Tell old Pharaoh,
Let my people go.

Letting go. Letting go of people. Letting go of reasons that have spoiled. Letting go of ideas that got stuck or just didn't work. Or changing them. Doesn't everything in God's world change?

I was a woman. A wife. Maybe more than anything else I was a wife. And a mother. Did I want to change that? I worked but I never went far. I worked at home and with the time that was left, I waited at home. Every day. One day after the other. Did I want to change that? Did I think I could? I don't know, but in later years I came to see that I was wrong. I came to know that women can be brave. They can see and they can travel. They can hear a voice and follow it. They can hear their own voice and follow it.

Prudence Crandall did. Saying no to her husband. Saying no to his ideas of Hell and damnation. Saying God is love.

Living in Illinois. Moving to Kansas. Reading, thinking, working, teaching, helping. Believing. And she was not silent.

"This is our land," Black Hawk, Chief of the Sauk Indians said. "We will fight to keep it."

"I am against the man who goes to war with the Indians," she said. "Indians need their land as much as we need ours."

"Black people are not citizens," Chief Supreme Court Justice Taney said. "They are inferior people and have no rights which the white man has to respect."

"I am saddened," she said, "that Judge Taney used the case of Crandall vs. the state of Connecticut to decide that Dred Scott was not a person, that he was just a piece of property and must be returned to slavery."

"We are going to John Brown's Kansas," blacks said as they left the plantations of Louisiana and Mississippi.

"I support the man who welcomes the Exodusters to Kansas," she said. "They are escaping southern cruelties, as if they were still slaves."

"Married women living in towns will be able to vote," a Kansas law said.

"Maybe it is the duty of women to be thankful for any little good," she said, "but I will fight on until all women can celebrate their emancipation."

"Prudence Crandall was right in teaching Negro children," the *Republican* newspaper said. "For over fifty years this disgrace has remained on our state," the *Times* agreed.

"I shall never plead poverty," she said. "My plea is for justice. It is a duty I owe myself and also to Connecticut to ask for redress for such slander and abuse as I have received at their hand."

Old and wrinkled, with one tooth in her mouth, saying, "I want to love everyone in the sense of the gospel, for true love never dies. It is as lasting as heaven."

Taking hold of her life, waving it like the white cheesecloth flag she carried, a symbol of peace. A reminder to the nations, to the people. And not turning away from the voice in her head. Following it. Her voice. Saying what she heard. Doing what she knew.

Yes, women can do that.

Lucy Stone did. Traveling from Boston to Rochester to Cincinnati to Louisville to Madison to Chicago to Pittsburgh to Harrisburgh to Cleveland to Dayton to Philadelphia to Wilmington to Ann Arbor to Denver to Fort Wayne to Richmond to Newark to Worcester to Saratoga Springs to Seneca Falls and yes, to Kansas. Writing, "There is no other name given, by which this country *can* be saved, but that of *woman*."

Sojourner Truth also took hold of her life. She said, "My name was Isabela, but when I left the house of bondage, I left everything behind. I wasn't going to keep anything of Egypt on me, and so I went to the Lord and asked him to give me a new name." Speaking, singing, writing. Singing the songs she wrote:

I am pleading for my people -
A poor, down-trodden race,
Who dwell in freedom's boasted land,
With no abiding place.

Whilst I bear upon my body
The scars of many a gash,
I am pleading for my people
Who groan beneath the lash.

I plead with you to sympathize
With sighs and groans and scars,
And note how base the tyranny
Beneath the stripes and stars.

And Mary Mountain did. A woman, a black woman, a woman of pleasure, who bought a horse, followed a map and traveled from a gold mining town in California to Boston to meet John, to give him money. "For your plan," she said. "For our freedom."

Were they dreaming? Were they crazy?

And one night Harriet had a dream. She was in a wilderness filled with rocks and bushes. Suddenly she saw a snake lift itself from behind a rock. Then, while she was looking at the snake, its head turned into a man's head. It was an old man's head with a white beard and sharp eyes. Hardly a minute later there were two other snakes. They were smaller and stayed close to the old man. And then from out of nowhere, men came. Soon there was a crowd. They gathered around the snakes, surrounding them. The old man looked at Harriet. He turned to her. He opened his mouth. He wanted to speak, but he was beaten and the smaller snakes were beaten too. They were beaten, the old man and the younger men, until they disappeared into the ground.

It was a clear day in April when John and Harriet met at her home in St. Catharines. She called him Captain Brown. He called her General Tubman. He told her his plan. "We will arm the slaves. We will help them escape to freedom." She told him about the land—where the mountain passes were, where the rivers could be crossed, where the forests and swamps were thick enough for shelter and for hiding. She told him where the friends of the Underground Railroad were. And what to say—"A friend with friends" when he knocked on the door. She told him the fastest, safest way to escape from Maryland, to escape from Harper's Ferry to the north. "I will draw you a map," she said.

And at that meeting, Harriet remembered the snake in her dream and she saw that the head of the snake, the head of that old man, was the head of my John, the head of John Brown.

CHAPTER 24

CRAZY.

Being crazy. Trying not to be crazy.

The poem Sarah made up:

There was an old woman who lived in a shoe
If you think that happened you're crazy too!

Teaching it to Ellen. Clapping hands. Pointing to their toes. Thinking it was funny, but not quite laughing. Smiling.

"You should be telling her stories from the Bible. You should be telling her stories of the prophets. You should be telling her stories of the Wise Men. You should be singing psalms, not nonsense."

They were looking at me.

"But it's not the Sabbath," Sarah said.

"Nonsense is nonsense no matter what day it is," I said, suddenly wondering if children needed nonsense, a little nonsense now and then, like a splash of color jumping up at you in the forest. But nonsense could also make you crazy. Talking nonsense. Believing nonsense. Acting crazy. And that was a sin—as if the sense God gave you wasn't good enough. As if you needed something more. As if you didn't trust Him. Denying His blessing. Destroying His image.

God created us in His own image; in the image of God He created us; male and female He created us.

Thinking about it. Pulled into it. The big hole of craziness. The falling into it. Hearing a voice. Having a dream. Does having a dream make you crazy? Or is it when you try to take the dream out of the night, away from the night, into the day? When you let your dream go into the world just as it is—naked? Trying to get past its nakedness, to make sense out of it?

Is that crazy?

Lifting the pot. Forgetting that it was hot. Dropping it—stew spilling to the floor. A potato on my shoe. A carrot under the table.

Annie came in.

"What's the matter? What happened?" she asked.

"I dropped the pot," I said.

Was that crazy?

Was I crazy?

Like John's grandmother?

Like Dianthe?

Like Johnny? Just that once—but maybe craziness is like that, going in and out of people like the breath of God. Going through a body and leaving no trace, no marker.

Like Frederick? But I wouldn't say that he was crazy—just when those headaches got to him or he had too much blood rushing around his head.

Like John?

And what's the difference between being crazy and being wrong?

Did anyone say I was crazy? Did anyone know I heard Dianthe's wolves howl? Did anyone know I looked at the stars and saw my children playing there? That sometimes I thought I could pick them up and dance with them? Did anyone know I bought a ribbon for my Sarah's hair and hid it in her coffin when she died? Did anyone know I wanted to lock Oliver in the shed because he was my youngest son, so eager, so hopeful, and I was afraid for him?

Did anyone know I said no to John when he asked me to go with him to Harper's Ferry?

CHAPTER 25

HOW DID HE DESCRIBE IT?

Two rivers, mountains rising from each. At the door of the black belt—the south and its sin of slavery, the south with its soul gone to Satan, the south and three million slaves.

"A road," he said. "It's a crossroad. One way to the south is where the slaves are. The other way to the north is where freedom is."

"A road?" I asked.

"Mountains that are as good as a road. Better than a road because there are places where run-aways can set up camp, even towns, and fortify themselves with food and weapons. Places where the brave and weary refugees can defend themselves and their families and wait for others to join them."

"How many others?" I asked. "Who will tell them to go? Who will tell them where to go? How to go? When to go? Who will help them to go? And weapons—where will they come from?"

"Can you imagine a black man defending his wife and children? Can you imagine a black man raising his head past another man's shadow? Raising his hands and his hopes the way other men do? Can you imagine a black man coming to his life, to his thinking and working the way other men do? Coming to God the way other men do? The gates will open, I tell you. The flood gates..."

"The gates?" I asked. "What gates?"

"Like dawn, like sunrise, the news will spread from mountaintop to mountaintop and down into the valleys, the towns and the plantations. They will come from Tennessee, and

Alabama, and Mississippi, and Georgia, and the Carolinas. The gates will open…"

I did not answer. In my head I could only see shiny, sturdy gates, the Heavenly Gates. Was that a meaning for life or death?

John opened his Bible and read, "The Spirit of the Lord God is upon me, because the Lord hath anointed me to preach good tidings unto the meek. He hath sent me to bind up the broken-hearted, to proclaim liberty to the captives, and the opening of the prison to them that are bound."

Was he right? Could it be? Was it meant to be? Was he a prophet? Could he be a savior?

"I am worried," I said, beginning slowly, because I was not sure of what I would say, because I was feeling that his words of righteousness and vision were grand, maybe even as grand as those of the patriarchs', but somehow not right. They were heavy. Too heavy for a man. For any man. Wondering if that is what Abraham's wife, Sarah, thought. Did she ever think that? Did she ever try to hold her husband back?

"The angel of the Lord will camp around me. The angel of the Lord will protect me. Show me the way. And," he added, "in just an hour's climb from Harper's Ferry, there is terrain that can hide a hundred men and more."

"Do you have a hundred men?" I asked.

"Is not this the fast that I have chosen? To loose the bands of wickedness, to undo the heavy burdens, and to let the oppressed go free, and that ye break every yoke?"

"John," I said, "you are not listening to me. You did not hear me. Do you have a hundred men?" I asked again.

"This is an age of miracles," he said. "But miracles don't happen by themselves. They need help."

He folded his arms. He lowered his voice. He looked at me—his John Brown look. The look I saw when I first said yes—and all the times after that.

"Will you help?" he asked.

Change. How does it happen? Holding on to a promise or letting go of it. But I had no choice. I could not say why I had to let go. Why I had to turn away from my husband, from our duties and purposes. I think I wanted to let things happen without me because I needed that. Because it was something I had become used to, the following along on the edge of the struggle for so long. Almost like holding on, holding on to the end of a rope, feeling its pull just barely. And now I was wanting to say no—for no sensible reason, just to say it, to hear it. What it would sound like—no... Would John understand that? Could he understand it if I couldn't? But didn't John always say that every person has a right to stand up for themselves? "Don't expect someone else to do what you can't do for yourself," he said.

Did I have a choice?

"Maybe," I said. "Maybe when the time comes. Maybe when the time is right if there is something I can do to help. Something more."

Thinking that perhaps John had no choice either, that he was latching on just as I was trying to let go. That he had to find answers for his questions and action for his words. That just as I needed to stand still, at least for a little while, he had to go forward.

And the others?

Thinking of Oliver first. So tall and strong. Remembering how he liked to wrestle. That spring day when he wrestled thirty lumbermen, one right after the other. Not that he was looking for a fight. He said it was like climbing a mountain, to see if he could do it. His dark hair still curly. But with John's eyes. So direct and keen.

Should I have said, "There are choices. For every yes there can be a no. And there are yes times and no times and sometimes it's not clear and sometimes you're not sure?" Should I have said, "There are living times and dying times?"

"The work is starting. The plan is going into action. The time is now. The waters are parting for us to cross, to bring our darker brothers and sisters to the Promised Land. Will you go with me?" John asked, looking at each of his sons. Looking at each of my sons.

Salmon answered first.

"I will not be a link in this chain. I cannot go," he said. "I've done all the warring and killing that I can do. I did it in Kansas. You know that I did. I stood by your side. But no more. Not again."

"Fighting is not for cowards," John said, staring at Salmon so hard that Salmon's eye began to twitch.

"Is fighting then for fools?" he asked.

"I am not a coward but I cannot go either," Henry said. "Surely to take care of one's farm and family is also God's work. That is what I think and that is what I will do. What I must do."

"God has only one face and one voice..." John began.

"And where would we be without Kansas? Without saving Lawrence and turning back the border ruffians? Without all the raids and battles, where would we be?" Owen asked. "We had to stand up, to plant our feet as firmly as our ideas. If we did not do that, if we closed our eyes and turned away, Kansas would be coming into the Union as a slave state and slavery would snake its way into all the Western territories."

Salmon spoke quietly. "Yes," he agreed, "I'll give you that father was right about Kansas. He knew what had to be done and we did what had to be done. But Harper's Ferry is not Kansas. Harper's Ferry is not Lawrence or Brown's Station. It's not the Battle of Black Jack. And it's not freeing a few slaves and taking them north. Can't you see that? The people are not ready. The slaves are not ready. There will be no support—not even an Indian to open his door to you, to give you some flour and eggs, some corn. And the mountains will not help you. They will trap you."

"I do not intend to be trapped," John said, as if he was saying something simple—like, listen to the bird singing or see how the stars twinkle.

"No one intends to be trapped, but you will be too cautious," Salmon insisted.

"I will strike when the time is right," he said, "just as I did in Kansas."

John stood up. A little stooped. His hair streaked gray. His short beard all gray. The Old Man. He looked like an old man. In Kansas they called him the Old Man. His sons all taller and stronger than he.

"Even the wise and wily fox gets trapped," Salmon continued. "And if the army comes..."

"And if the army doesn't come? And if we can free some slaves?" Oliver asked.

"Besides, the downfall of slavery is laid as much on our souls as it is on father's," Watson said. "And if it should come to that, if Harper's Ferry is a trap, I will not let father die alone."

So there it was. The lines drawn. Some on one side. Some on the other. I wasn't surprised. They were never afraid to listen, to speak, to argue, to disagree. But who was right?

And Oliver newly married, falling in love and marrying Martha, who was young, just seventeen, as I was when I married John. And strong. Strong enough to leave her family. Strong enough to stand next to Oliver, to give him her future. Strong... but yes, what else could she do? A woman—she could not make her life, she found it and had to live it.

"Don't marry into that Brown family," Martha's folks had said. "They're too high on Abolition. Too deep into it to ever pull themselves out."

Standing close to each other. Sitting close to each other. Touching sometimes. Racing to the knoll to watch the sun set. Talking sometimes.

And then, "There will be a baby in the new year," Martha said.

Babies. Once again babies. Always babies. Do they ever leave you? Thinking about my first baby. After so many years, so many twists and turns, I could still feel my first baby, my first Sarah. I could still see her big eyes and big tears when she cried. And all the babies. I could see and feel and hear all the babies that died and the babies that lived, that had grown and were living.

Oliver calling the family together. Telling Ruth and her husband, Henry, and Owen and Salmon and his wife, Abbie, and Watson and his wife, Belle, and Annie and Sarah and Ellen—picking Ellen up and swinging her so high, so fast she almost cried. Writing to Johnny and Jase. Telling John and me.

"There will be a baby," he said. "There will be a baby." And there were little crinkles around his eyes, as if they were smiling.

But he went. When the time came, he left Martha and went

with John and Owen to Harper's Ferry.

Writing to his wife, "Don't worry. The plan is simple and safe and we are drilled and well-prepared. We study maps, we read our arms manual and the manual of military tactics. And we have 950 pikes, 2000 revolvers and 198 Sharps repeating rifles."

And again, "Don't worry. A few good men in the right and knowing they are right, can overturn a king. Also there is a truly fine marksman among us. He can shoot tacks into a tree from a far distance. I've seen him do it many times. And, for an extra, he is also a poet. Maybe he will write a poem that I can send you."

And Oliver's last letter, "You can hardly think how lonesome it was the day I left you. Also forgive me but I feel compelled to say that I have a great anxiety about you in your present condition. Let me ask you to try to keep up good, cheerful spirits, take plenty of sleep and rest and plenty of out-door-exercise. Make the most of everything. Heaven bless you, my dear Martha, and remember your affectionate husband."

And Martha answered, "I'm sure all the men in your company are good and true, but I know who is the best and the bravest, and it is you, my beloved, who I hold in my heart day and night, and that makes me the happiest."

Then it was Watson's turn. He cried, his sobs filled the house, but he left his wife and his baby, just two weeks old. Joining Oliver and Owen and John at Harper's Ferry, and the eighteen other men.

Watson writing to his wife, "I would gladly come home and stay with you always, but for that which brought me here—a desire to do something for others, and not to live wholly for my own happiness. "

Writing, "There was a slave near here whose wife was sold off South and he was found in his master's orchard, dead, the next morning. How can I come home so long as such things are done?"

Writing, "I sometimes think perhaps we shall not meet again. If we should not, you have an object to live for... to be a mother to our little Fred. And remember to give him a kiss from his father every night."

And Belle answered, "I pray every day that you will come back as soon as possible, then you will be able to kiss our son yourself. Dearest, I think of you all night in my dreams and wait for you every day. It is all that I live for."

And Watson's last letter, "O, Belle, I would give a good deal for your picture. Give my regards to all the friends and know there is a better day a-coming. Believe me yours wholly and forever in love."

Twenty-two men. Twenty-two men. How could that be enough?

"If God be for us, who can be against us?" John had asked. "And more men are coming, from Canada and Kansas and Iowa."

And then the letter from John. The choice made real. Offered again. Like a prayer. Offered again. Like a sacrifice. Thinking of the patriarchs again. Thinking of Sarah. Did she say, "No, don't take Isaac. Your voices are not my voices. Your vision is not my vision. And he is my son"?

No, she said nothing because she knew nothing, not knowing that her son was to be sacrificed. Not knowing that she was to be sacrificed through her son. The inkling of Jesus to come. The sacrifice—and the glory of Mary.

He wrote, "I would be most glad to have you and Annie come on and make me a visit of a few weeks. I find it will be indispensable to have some women of our own family with us for a short time. I don't see how I can get along without, and on that account I have sent Oliver at a good deal of expense to come back with you; and if you cannot come, I would be glad to have Martha and Annie come on. But you will have no more exposure here than at North Elba, and you can return after a short visit. Mary, I want you to come right off. It will likely prove the most valuable service you can ever render to the world."

Reading the letter over and over.

Why did my legs drag about like stone? Why did my heart sink away in my chest, as deep as a stone dropped into a well?

To be with my husband. To work with him. To help him. To feed him. To sleep with him. To be a wife and to sleep with him...

I closed my eyes.

"I wish you health and success in the great and good cause you are engaged in," I wrote, "but I am not well. The time is not right. I cannot leave Ellen. I cannot go."

Annie, writing in her large firm hand, saying that she was willing to go. "As soon as Oliver comes for us, I will be ready."

"And I, "Martha added, "am already packed and will be ready even sooner. It will be like a paradise to be with my husband, to help him and you engage in this fight and finish it for the good."

The year was 1859.

John was gone.

Owen was gone.

Watson was gone.

Oliver was gone.

Martha and Annie were gone.

And the summer–June, July and August were gone. Then September and another letter from John.

"Martha and Annie are well and will be on the way home in the course of this month as our plans go forward," he wrote. "But I do not know what to advise about the spotted cow as much will depend on what you have to feed her."

And then the end of September when Martha and Annie did come home. Returning with the chill–no, the cold–already down from the mountains, the sun shining through bare trees and almost bare trees, making shadows and angles, so many, so sharp and twisted. Returning with the smaller, darker days.

And the next letter from John, his last letter.

"Dear Wife and children, all," he wrote. "You can keep the animals in good condition through the winter on potatoes mostly, which is much cheaper than any other feed, especially if the crop is good and secured well and in time.

"I am sending home four blankets. They are for Martha, Belle, Annie and Abbie. Martha should have the first choice because of her particular condition. To my other daughters I can only send my blessing just now."

And the lines to Annie, "I want you, first of all, to become a sincere, humble, earnest and consistent Christian; and then acquire good and efficient business habits. And it would be worthwhile if you could save this letter to remember your father by."

And then the lines for me, "Mary, I have encouragement of having fifty dollars or more to be sent to you soon, to get you through the winter. And I shall certainly do all in my power for you, and try to commend you always to the God of my fathers."

Was that the beginning? The beginning of good news?

A household of women. Six women. Praying together every morning and every night. And before we said Amen, we sang one of the songs that the men sang as they were waiting. Singing Nearer My God To Thee or The Slave Has Seen The North Star or All The Dear Folks Have Gone. We even sang Faded Flowers.

"It's true that they sang," Martha said that first evening she was home. "And Charles and Aaron had such good deep voices. If I close my eyes I can hear them even now."

Annie began to hum. "They would sing as if they were around a campfire," she said. "At least, that's what they wanted to do. I always had to quiet them. 'You'll wake the walls,' I used to say."

Belle got up to tend to her baby.

Sarah brought cookies to the table and gave one to Ellen.

"But it was hard," Martha continued. "So many men in one house. And they couldn't go out. They couldn't make noise. Almost always together. Telling stories, reading the newspaper, sometimes a book–John Kagi was reading The Age Of Reason, so much arguing for and against it."

"If you can imagine that," Annie said, folding her arms across her chest, as John might do. "Arguing night after night because Mr. Paine didn't believe in any church at all. He believed in the equality of men, but he said that churches were human inventions and that his mind was his church!"

"And father let him say that?" Abbie asked.

"And reading letters," Martha said. "Of course, they did that. Dangerfield reading the letters from his wife asking, 'My dear husband, when will you come to get me? When will you free me and the children?' Begging, 'My dear husband, you must come soon, before it is too late and I am sold south.' Edwin and Barclay reading the letter from their mother asking, 'When thou gettest halters around thy necks, wilt thou think of me?'

"The men writing letters.

"Barclay writing to his mother, 'We cannot die in a better cause.' John Anthony writing to his parents, 'Remember the cause I am engaged in is a Holy Cause.' Jeremiah writing to his sweetheart, Jennie, 'What happiness there is in thinking and knowing that we are doing the best we can for the good of humanity.'

"And because the days were so long and the nights even longer, the men played cards and checkers. Jumping up and down for exercise. Sometimes helping with the chores. Sometimes going out, one by one, to the post office or the store. But mostly, of course, they had to hide."

"Especially when that barefoot, old Mrs. Huffmaster came by," Annie said, lowering her voice almost to a whisper. "She was a plague worse than fleas. Coming around at all hours of the day and we were afraid she would find us out and betray us. It was like standing on a powder magazine after a slow match has been lighted. And when she came near, I would give the word, and if the men were in the dining room, quick as a wink they would clear the food from the table, speed up to the attic and come back down when she was gone."

"I called her the hen with her little chicks because she always had a flock of children with her," Martha said. "And she would have been funny if she wasn't dangerous.

"'Always washing clothes, are you?' she asked. 'Is that a family or an army you have in your house? Tell me again, what did you say you were all doing down here?'

"And then there was the time father and Annie were away, going down the road to that good German church and no one was on the lookout and Mrs. Huffmaster just came right into the farmhouse and Shields Green was there and she saw him.

"'Feeding a nigger, are you, same as if he was a white man?'

she asked. 'He's a run-off slave you're keeping here, isn't he?' She put her hands on her hips. 'Now isn't that something—stealing and running slaves away.'

"'Mrs. Huffmaster, you are plain silly and wrong as a blue cow,' I said, giving her children chunks of the bread I had just baked. 'Now what in the world would we be doing with slaves? He's just a hired hand to help get the house in order, to fix it up for our mother's arrival.'

"Of course, it wasn't only Mrs. Huffmaster," Martha continued. "Other people were getting suspicious. Neighbors. Men in town. Farmers. Asking questions. 'Why does your wagon go into town every day? What load is in it? When did you say your mother was coming?'"

"And then," Annie said, "there was the time Shields was away from the house. He had gone with Owen to Chambersburg and they were returning when someone saw him, called to him to stop, began to chase him. Running, zigzagging, dodging through forest and cornfield. Then they came to a river and Owen jumped in but Shields stopped on the bank. They could hear horses behind them. They could hear men beating the brush.

"'Hurry up,' Owen said. 'Jump in.'

"'There's no way I'm going to do that,' Shields answered, 'because it happens that I can't swim. And the good Lord knows for sure what a poor fool I am. I've got myself out of slavery, all the way from South Carolina without swimming a stroke and here I am facing a river and back in the eagle's claw again.'

"'I wouldn't go that far,' Owen said, climbing out of the river, back up the bank. 'The eagle is just circling and it hasn't got you yet. And there's more than one way to cross the river. So I'll be the ship and you can be the sailor. Just get on my back and we'll get across."

I put more wood on the fire. Ellen and Sarah sat close to it.

"Surely that was a good sign," I said. "Father often talks about crossing the river to safety, crossing the river to safety as the Israelites did."

"Yes, maybe it was a good sign," Annie continued, "because they did get across the river. And then they turned south but their pursuers thought they would go north..."

"And they escaped?" I asked.

Annie nodded. Fire shadows on her face.

"The justice of it," I said. "A white man and a black man out-thinking those southerners. As sure as anything, that day with its river was a good sign."

Looking for good signs. What was wrong with that?

"And what do you think about birds?" Annie asked. "Can they be a sign?"

"Anything can be a sign," Abbie said, helping Ellen to climb onto her lap, hugging her, rocking her.

"A bird. A little yellow bird..." I said too softly for anyone to hear.

"What happened with birds?" Belle asked, putting her baby back in the cradle.

"Father and I were sitting on the porch," Annie continued. "He was worried because he didn't know how many men he would have, how many men would go with him to Harper's Ferry. And I was telling him that I could ride and I could shoot. I was telling him that I could be another man in his army, but he wasn't listening to me. He was looking at something and when I followed his gaze I saw that he was watching two wrens that were flying nearby. They were flying up and down. Up and down. Again and again. Beating their wings and twittering.

"'What do they want?" father asked. 'Why are they doing that? What do you think they want?"

"I shook my head. 'I don't know,' I said. 'Is it a sickness? A craziness? Attracting so much attention when they should be hiding.'

"'They must know something. They must want something. The way they are almost pointing. The way they are almost shrieking. What could it be? What could they want?'

"What was it?" Sarah asked, taking another cookie. "What was it?"

"Well, father went off the porch, trying to follow their lead."

"And did he find something?" Abbie asked.

"Yes he did. He followed the birds and he found their nest.

But he also found something else."

"What was it?" Sarah asked again. "What was it?"

"Father found a snake right there by the nest. It was coiled and ready to strike. And just as calm as anything, he got a long stout stick and killed the snake. And when he came back he was smiling and do you know what he said?"

"What?" we all asked, almost together.

He looked up at the blue shadows of the mountains and said, 'For now we live, if ye stand fast in the Lord.'"

"Amen," I said.

And then the others–"Amen." "Amen." "Amen." "Amen." "Amen." Even little Ellen saying, "Amen for grandfather. Amen."

Good news. Good omens.

But not always. Not often enough. Only sometimes. Not day after day. Of course, not–how could I think that? The days with no night between them.

"There were rumors," Martha said. "This was going to happen and that was going to happen. It was like we were in a net, being caught in a net, being pulled in. It was terrible... And then Dangerfield came in one night and said, 'People are angry. They think our wagon carries guns from the arsenal for fugitive slaves. There is talk of searching the house.'

"Owen agreed. 'Even Mr. Unseld rides close to us. Tries to look into the wagon. Asking, Is it wool you're carrying? And where are the sheep?'

"'They are closing in on us,' father said. 'It is time to act. Time to move against the arsenal. No time to dally, we must move quickly.' And that's when he sent us home. "And going home wasn't just going for an afternoon ride," Annie said. "We were in the wagon on the great pike to Harrisburg, when we heard the pounding of a horse riding madly, coming toward us, almost on top of us. Passing us close by, but then turning back and riding behind the wagon, next to Watson. Riding for some time. Saying nothing."

"Since I was a little girl, it's the most scared I've ever been," Martha said. "But Oliver was driving the mule and we just kept on going at a smooth and steady pace."

"Then we heard the man ask, 'What are you carrying in there?' And before Watson could answer, the man threw open the back flap of the canvas cover. And there we were. Trying to sit as neat and proper as we could.

"He sort of blinked when he saw us, taking off his hat and bowing his head politely. 'Excuse me ladies,' he said. 'I didn't know you were in there.'"

"So father was right again," Martha said. "They were closing in on us. And we -they, our men have to show their hand before it is taken from them. Before the net is closed..."

The fire was dying. Ellen had fallen asleep on Abbie's lap. I took her and Abbie got up to bank the fire.

Martha was sipping some warm milk. "To make my baby strong," she said. "It will be a boy. A son for Oliver."

Sarah was moving toward bed. Ellen was warm against me.

"And we must wait," I said. "They will move. Maybe thay are moving right at this moment, but we will wait. We have to wait for..."

I didn't know for what.

Yes, the wait, the weight of women... But how does it happen that a bullet can go through a mother's son? And a husband...

CHAPTER 26

"DEAR CHILDREN, ONE AND ALL,

I have arrived and expect to stay here with Mrs. Mott until—how can I say it?—until your father is disposed of. I don't know, are there other words that could say it better? Other words that could say it dearer? Make it easier? Other words that could undo this terrible thing? But your father says we should not feel shame because of him. We should not feel degraded or outcast because of him. He says it should be with gratitude that we receive all that our Father in heaven may send us, for He doeth all things well. And he writes that he is not only tranquil but joyous. So may the God of all peace be with us as He is with him."

Watching the words fill the paper. So many words and yet so much more to say.

"I know it has only been a few days, but it seems a great while since I have seen you. I hope you have written so I can hear from you. Ellen, how are you doing? I hope you are a good. And I hope to see you all before very long."

So I stayed with Lucretia Mott. And I dreamed.

In a few days, John would say how beautiful it all was—the world, as if he was just waking up and looking, without hurry or purpose, for the first time. Seeing the world. Loving it... The fields sweeping between the river and the mountains, almost golden in the sun that would soon turn to winter.

"This is a beautiful country," John would say. "I never had the pleasure of seeing it before."

Lucretia showing me to my room. Her hand reaching up to my shoulder.

"This is your room," she was saying. "Stay as long as you like. As long as you need to."

In a room by myself. At the end of the hall, in the back of the house, close to the gardens. A breeze drifting through the leafless trees, fluttering the corn shocks. A cow in the distance. A horse. A dog barking. A woodpecker—I'm sure I heard a woodpecker, probably banging its head at that old apple tree by the front fence.

The first time I was to stay in a room by myself. A poem stitched and hanging on the wall:

If slavery comes by color,
which God gave,
Fashion may change,
and you become the slave.

Dreaming, I should have dreamed of terror, of fear, of loneliness, of cold—even of hunger and pain and death. I should have seen the cold and dark of the engine house. I should have heard Oliver cry out again and again. I should have heard and remembered his silence. And then Watson.

"What brought you here?" he was asked.

"My duty, sir," he answered.

Oliver and Watson side by side on the engine house floor. In Harper's Ferry.

But I dreamed of a house. A great house with wide windows and doors. A great house with shiny wood floors and warm rugs. A great house with a sturdy porch and a view from every angle. One room leading to another, so many rooms, I never did get the count straight. Twenty two? Twenty three? Twenty four? So many rooms, I never walked through the same room twice. Or if I did, it was changed somehow, so that I didn't know it was the room I had been in before.

Only the house. No furniture. No people.

Did I live there? In that house? In this or that room—with no spinning wheel, no loom, no cradle?

And where was John?

A great house with a wide green lawn. Getting smaller and

smaller the closer I came to it. Rooms dropping away, disappearing, crumbling as if the house, as great as it was, was nothing but a loaf, a cake, long since dried up. Rooms getting smaller and smaller. One room. So small how could anyone fit in it? Just big enough for a person. For one person. To lie down in. Small enough or big enough to collect letters. All the letters that had come and gone. All the letters that were coming and going.

"If you feel sure you can endure the trials and the shock which will be unavoidable, I should be glad to see you once more," John wrote, "but when I think of you being insulted on the road, and perhaps while here, and of only seeing your wretchedness made complete, I shrink from it."

Wretchedness? I did not think of myself as being wretched. Blessed?

"I am blessed," John's sister wrote. "I am blessed and I rejoice that a brother of mine is accounted worthy to suffer and die in His cause."

No, I did not think of myself as either blessed or chosen. I thought of myself as being sheared like a sheep, as being bare like a tree, as being—like the house in my dreams, crumbling...

The train from Philadelphia to Harper's Ferry. A closed carriage to Charlestown.

The shout from the road, "Ain't the old turkey buzzard dead yet?"

I drew the curtains, seeing only the sergeant and the soldiers riding alongside. And the gray beyond.

"It's some kind of crazy fool that can't tell a turkey buzzard from an eagle," I said to myself. "An eagle spreading his wings. Soon to fly."

And the words themselves were light and feathery and seemed to fly—briefly, until I was brought back to other words.

"Sir, it is my wish to make a decent burial for my husband and my sons, to have a decent and tender interment among their kindred."

"Madam, we shall deliver the mortal remains of your husband when all shall be over."

"And my sons?"

"Madam, they were raiders, rebels, robbers..."

"And my sons?" I repeated.

"Your sons have been buried like the others. Some in the same box. In the woods on the other side of the Shenandoah, with no markers..."

The carriage turning, slowing down. Passing other carriages. Passing soldiers on horseback and marching soldiers. A military band playing. The sun slanting through the clouds.

And then the jail, as if it was a jewel set and held by the stony faces of soldier after soldier. A thousand soldiers, I was told, their bayonets suddenly, all at once, glistening in the sun. And cannon. Seven brass cannon facing the jail.

"I am Mrs. Brown," I said to the jailer.

"Yes, ma'am, I was told to expect you," he said. "I know it has been a difficult journey..."

Listening. The way he took so long with every word. Talking the way southerners do.

Calling to his wife. "Mrs. Brown has arrived," he said. And then, "I'll be outside the door. Let me know when you are done."

The wife saying, "Mrs. Brown, this is something I have to do." Patting my chest, my stomach, my back, looking to see if there were hidden pockets in my skirt, lifting my skirt.

"Mrs. Brown, do you have a knife? Mrs. Brown, do you have any strychnine? Mrs. Brown, this is something I have to ask," she said.

I shook my head.

"You are thinking that Mr. Brown plans to escape as if he was a criminal. But he is not a criminal and he has no wish to escape or to cheat the gallows," I said, the words rushing past me, as if they were saying themselves. "So you are wrong and all those soldiers with their guns and bayonets are wrong. My husband is not a criminal and he is not a victim. He is a prophet and an apostle for Christ. He is suffering for the truth and the love of God and he is grateful for it."

She touched my hand for a moment, turned, murmured

something and opened the door.

"It's been done," she told her husband.

"Please, Mrs. Brown, follow me," the jailer said. And again, "This way, Mrs. Brown."

Following him through one room and then another. Feeling the cold, the damp, the dark. And then a room—no, not a room, a cell. The jailer fitting the key into the lock. The sound of the key pushed into the lock. The door swinging open. The sound of the door opening. That sound... I can hear it...

"John."

"Mary."

Coming together. Squeezing a lifetime between us. Trying to hold onto it. Trying to hold onto each other.

"John... What is there to say when everything must be said at once..."

"Mary," he asked, his finger slowly tracing a still red scar across his forehead, "do you think I have failed?"

"Failed?" I hesitated. "Failed? Does a river fail? Does a mountain fail? Do the stars fail when they are clouded over? And surely you have read the papers and know..."

"Yes," he interrupted, nodding toward the jailer. "Yes, my keeper is a gentleman and I have been well provided with papers and with news and with letters of encouragement."

"Have there been many?" I asked.

"As many as I could have hoped for. More than I could have hoped for. And have you heard the little ditty that is being sung?"

He did not wait for me to answer.

There's a flutter in the Southland, a tremor in the air,
For the rice plains are invaded, the cotton fields laid bare,
And the cry of "help" and "treason" rings loud from tongue and pen,
John Brown has crossed the border with a host of fifteen men.

He smiled. I smiled. Smiling in a jail—for a moment. Just for a moment. Smiling until he shuffled his feet, turned, walking slowly to his writing table. The chains, his chains pulling across the cold bare floor. What was the reason for chains around his sore and swollen ankles? Was it thought that he would run away, through the locked door, the brick walls, past the soldiers and the mob, through the town, to the mountains? Was it thought that he could?

Quiet for a few moments. Maybe longer than that. Maybe shorter. The jailer, standing by the door. His breathing coming between us. His cough. And the General was there too.

Then John said, "But you are right. It is too late for questions. It is the time for answers. The Captain of my salvation has taken away my sword of steel and put into my hands a sword of spirit. And I am ready and I will answer with my life."

He turned to his desk and found the letters he was looking for. He opened one, taking out a $100 check, endorsing it and giving it to me. He opened another letter, taking out a $50 check, endorsing it and giving it to me.

"Yes, offers of help have come to me too, from friends that we know and friends that we don't know. But, John, it is charity..."

"Charity is not always what it seems. Sometimes it is payment," he said. "Besides, the sympathy that is aroused in your behalf today or tomorrow may not always follow you. Helping poor widows and children is about as romantic as helping the so-called nigger. Both are easily forgotten."

Silence again. And floating into that silence, the house in North Elba. The door, Martha so big with child, standing to the side. Belle, holding little Fred, trying to hush his crying. Annie and Sarah and Ellen standing together, almost in a circle, almost huddled together in a circle. Ellen, holding the bible John had given her, crying, "Mother. Mother. Mother." Looking back, into another world. Seeing them so large in front of the house and then so small. A smudge in front of a house, in front of the mountains.

The children. My God, the children.

"John, oh John, it is so hard. It is such a hard fate. Our poor children... What will become of them?"

"What will become of them is in God's hands. All we can

do is be of good cheer and bear this in the best manner we can. You must help the children to see the glory in the sorrow, the joy in the turmoil. You have to bring them to God, to see His light, to walk in His way. Then they will feel strong and sure. And they will feel safe. Even in this world of sin and sorrow they will feel safe."

He lowered his voice, shuffled his weight from one leg to the other, walking... And again the chains, a crashing sound, thundering like a mighty waterfall.

"You know, of course, it was my will to come home. It was my hope to come home and to send my sons home to their wives. To send all my men home to those who were waiting for them and praying for them. But I am fulfilling the Lord's will, not my own. So you must tell our children that it is all for the best. Tell them that I have never seen a night so dark as to have hindered the coming day. Tell them that their father died without a single regret for the course he has pursued. Tell them that we will all meet in Heaven with our Father, where all are at peace and are free."

The cell door opening. Whispers. The jailer whispering to his wife. The jailer whispering to the General.

"There is food," the jailer said.

We walked to the parlor. A short walk. We walked, walking arm in arm. To the table–seeing that it was set for one.

"Why is the table set for one?" I asked.

"Mr. Brown is not permitted to use utensils," the jailer answered.

"Are you afraid that he will stab himself with a fork or spoon?"

"It is alright, Mary. The jailer must do what he must do. And I don't mind. I'm not hungry," John said, nibbling a roll and then a potato spud.

"And what of the boys? Oliver and Watson?" he asked.

"I don't know. I have asked....for their bodies. But there is no marker where they are buried. The boxes would have to be found. Dug up. I would have to look through boxes. Box after box. Body after body. And Governor Wise informs me that the bodies may have rotted..." I shuddered. The tears in my eyes turned John into a blur. I wiped my eyes. I took a deep breath.

"I think If you can get the boys, it would be good. Getting their bodies and mine and the Thompson brothers, and maybe all the raiders. Then you can burn the bodies on a pile of pine logs...."

"Impossible," the General interrupted. He was not whispering. "That is out of the question without a doubt. The laws of the state of Virginia would not permit such sacrilege."

"John," I said, my voice shaking, "do not ask it. It is more than I can do."

He reached out. He put his hands on my shoulders, slid them down my arms, resting on my waist. "Don't fret," he said, "I just thought the plan would save money and be the best." And then a question or two. Instructions for doing this or that. The money from father's estate is to be equally divided. Give the girls a plain but practical education. Give bibles to everyone. Take care of yourself and the house. Live in the house. Remember always to love God and to walk in His ways.

And then it was time to go. No, it wasn't that it was time to go, but that the General said, "The visit has lasted longer than was planned. We have a long ride back to Harper's Ferry. It is time to go."

"Can Mrs. Brown spend the night?" John asked.

"That is beyond the scope of my orders," the General said. "Alright then," John answered. "I have asked no favors from the state of Virginia and I will ask none now."

We looked at each other. Coming close to each other again. I reached up and touched the scar on his forehead. I let my hand rumple through his beard. Smooth it.

"In Heaven, my dear and devoted wife, until we meet in Heaven," he said.

At least, I think that is what he said. Leaving the jail. Leaving John. So hard to remember exactly what was said. Wondering if that was the way it had to be. Thinking if John hadn't looked back when he was in the engine house. What would have happened if he wasn't worried about his prisoners? If he wasn't worried about the wounded and the dying? Thinking if he wasn't worried, he could have escaped. There was time. Everyone said so. But he didn't look forward. And now I was the one who was looking forward. I was the one who had to look forward. As if we had changed places. As if I was Lot, going forward to a new place. Was there a meaning in that?

Coming back to Harper's Ferry. Miller McKim and his wife, Sarah, greeting me, walking me to my hotel room.

Once again in a room by myself. A view from the window? Was there a view? To one side the Blue Ridge Mountains. To the other side the square. Too dark to see the blood soaked stones. Too dark to see...

Too dark and yet there was no night. There was no sleep. No rest. No dream. There were shadows—but so thin and poor I couldn't make them out.

And then it was daybreak. Daylight. And colors came from out of nowhere. Mrs. McKim knocking on the door.

"Mrs. Brown would you care to join us for breakfast?"

"No."

What else could I say? Could I say I wanted to feel empty? That I did feel an emptiness that food could not fill? Would she understand—that I had to have that emptiness? That I had to hold onto that? Like a rock in my heart? That that was all I had...until I had the body of my husband?

I wanted to wait. Quietly. Alone. Would I know when it was done? Would I feel it in my bones, see it in my head—with my eyes opened or closed, touch it on my pillow, smell it on my handkerchief... when John walked up the steps to the scaffold? How many steps were there? Would he count them? Would he still be chained—to the last? And would he smile? Would he say a prayer? Would he say goodbye? Would he call my name? Would he think it?

The day was Friday. The time was 11:30 A.M. It was warm for this time of the year. The sun was shining. And John Brown had climbed the scaffold steps. And John Brown was swinging over the scaffold. And John Brown was hanging. And John Brown was dangling between Heaven and earth.

John Brown was dead.

The jailer helped to put his body in a coffin, a black coffin. He helped to load it onto the wagon. The wagon, the jailer and the coffin arriving in Harper's Ferry at 6 P.M. Just after sunset.

And then the journey home. From Harper's Ferry to Baltimore. From Baltimore to Philadelphia.

"Can we stop here? Can we have the body embalmed?"

Fifty members of the Shiloh Baptist Colored Church had come to the station. They would escort the coffin.

But also crowds of people, blacks and whites. Angry and sad. Mobs.

"No," the mayor said. "No telling what might happen."

Waiting until the people had gone, wrapping the coffin in an old blanket, slipping it into a run-down wagon and taking it to the wharf for the trip to New York City. Staying the night in New York City.

"I do not want my husband to be buried in a southern coffin."

The southern coffin changed for a northern one. His hanging clothes changed to a pleated white shroud with a white cravat.

"I do not want any demonstrations or eulogies. We must get home as soon as possible."

From New York City to Troy. Knowing that would be hard.

"Stay at the American House," John had told me.

Coming to the American House. Seeing my husband. Seeing my sons. Seeing Oliver help Martha down from the wagon on that last trip. Kissing her. Putting a lock of her hair in his pocket. Saying goodbye. Saying he would see her soon. Telling her to take care. Telling her to be brave.

From Troy to Rutland. From Rutland to Vergennes. From Vergeness moving down the road, approaching the lake, along the bridge by Otter Creek, men lining the road, removing their hats in the driving rain and sleet. Across Lake Champlain, the wind whipping the water over the thin sheets of ice, to Westport.

"We cannot go on as planned. Rain wiping out the snow. Sleighs have to be changed for wagons."

Boarding the wagons. Horses pulling slowly. Plodding.

Passing the arena of the Essex County Fair where John had shown his sheep. Where he had won prizes.

"We did not think that Virginia would do the bloody deed."

From Westport to Elizabethtown. The coffin taken to the Courthouse.

"We would be pleased to stand watch over the coffin until dawn."

And the next day's journey. The last twenty five miles. Slipping back, going forward. Climbing.

"Too steep and slippery, The horses have to be changed for oxen, Mrs. Brown."

Climbing the mountain pass. Almost inch by inch. Bouncing. Lurching. Into the wind and rain. Descending to the other side.

So many trains. So many boats. So many wagons. So many miles. So many cities. And the people—so many people, helping, bringing food, bringing blankets, an extra pair of boots. And always the bells. Wherever we went it seemed there were always bells. Always ringing.

And now, suddenly it was quiet. The wagon had slowed and stopped for the last time.

And through the quiet I could hear Annie call to me, "Mama. Mama," she was saying.

And through the quiet I called to her. "Annie. Oh, Annie," I said.

CHAPTER 27

AND THAT WAS THAT.

Stone is stone. And water is water. And my head was a mountain–jagged and shear, like Whiteface, like Mt. Marcy. Looking at them so long.

This night, this night that had been coming for so many years, was here, coming down, swooping down. A black bird just coming, covering, burying everything in its black coldness and thick darkness.

Hearing a whisper. A refrain. *Blow Ye The Trumpets Blow...* Whose voice? Whose voice did I hear? Listening but so hard to tell. Sarah? Was it Sarah? Was she leading the little ones–a chorus, the way she liked to do? Strands separating. Becoming clearer, but not so clear. Was it Watson and Oliver when they were small? Their silvery voices growing round and deep, growing into voices that could find their way around falsehood and through sin and above darkness. Growing into voices that could reach beyond themselves, that could say goodbye when they had to say goodbye.

Or was it Owen's voice? Running away from Harper's Ferry. Fleeing. Hiding and hunted, had he been found?

Or was it John who was singing? Or Dianthe?

Sleeping in my own house, in my own bed. A sore muscle in my shoulder. A cramp in my leg. A pain in my chest. A tightness in my stomach. And then, as if that wasn't enough, the monthlies–blood, warm blood seeping, between my legs.

"His gallows will be the emblem of a second Savior, whose sacrificial blood has ransomed the black man," it was written.

I was embarrassed–forty-three years old and I was caught

like a young girl. Fumbling in the darkness for a cloth. Wiping the sheet. Trying to wipe the sheet without waking Annie. Folding the cloth between my legs. The way life needed to be tended to, intruding itself just as it pleased. As if nothing else mattered. As if life was all that there was.

Death? Haven't you heard about death?

"Mother, are you alright?" Annie asked, turning over, sitting up in bed.

"John Brown was one bright, clear flash and that flash will run from man to man, from town to town across a South that will soon be drenched with blood," it was written.

Martha had fallen asleep in the arm chair, her legs stretched out on a pillow. Sitting so close to the coffin, her shadow fell across it. The glass of unfinished milk on the floor.

"I need to be near... something," she said. "I need to be near the coffin. To be able to touch it."

Fred starting to fuss and Belle got up, found another blanket and began to wrap it around him Indian style.

"Why are you doing that?" I asked. "If you catch him up so tight, he won't be able to move."

"He doesn't have to," Belle answered, lifting her nightshirt to him, holding him close to her, kissing him on the cheek, on the forehead—once, twice, and again.

Then Ellen calling "Mother," pulled her blanket with her and climbed into my bed. A few minutes later, Sarah, who was shivering with the cold, came too.

Abbie waking up.

"Ellen can sleep with us," she said.

But Ellen was already squirreled into the bed, both her hands holding onto my arm, pulling my hands to her face. Covering her face.

Annie got up to sleep in Sarah and Ellen's bed. Then went stumbling to the chest looking for another blanket.

"He sleeps in the blessings of the crushed and the poor and men believe more firmly in virtue because such a man has lived," it was written.

Putting my hand between my legs. All the way up between my legs. Feeling the cloth, warm, moist. When would this bleeding stop? Wasn't it time for my old body to give up? To stop pretending it was young? To stop pretending it was strong?

Someone was stirring upstairs. Mr. Phillips? Mr. McKim? The Reverend Mr. Joshua Young? Was he saying the prayer that he would say tomorrow?

"Though his body fall, the spirit of slavery and despotism falls with it, while John Brown goes up to Heaven. Let cherubic legions attend him. Let seraphims of glory be about him," it was written.

And Mr. Higginson? He did not come.

"You have been a loyal and generous friend for so long, will you come to the funeral?" I asked.

He frowned.

"Your husband is a hero," he said. "He is a hero and a martyr and he deserves a martyr's shrine."

"Perhaps..." I began. "But I am a plain woman and I don't know that much about heroes and martyrs. What I know is that my husband was a lamb unto his God. That he strived to be a man unto his fellow man."

"And so he was. But how will his fellow man come to pay their respects? Do you think they will hazard a journey across the mountains to this no-man's land? He will soon be forgotten. John Brown... not even a whisper in the wind. His death will have no meaning, it will have been in vain."

Finally, I was understanding the reason of his excitement, swinging his arms back and forth as if that would swing me to his meaning.

"I don't think you understand," I said. "John traveled the country, up and down, many times, and he traveled the world too, but this was his home. His dreams were here and, if he had lived, his future would have been here too. And if he would have been here in his life, so will he be here in his death."

"Boston..." he began.

"Yes, I know there are people, many people in Boston..."

"Hundreds of people. Thousands of people. And they come from the south and the west. And there are old churches and grand cemeteries and trains to go from one place to another even in the winter..."

I waited for him to look at me directly.

"But, Mr. Higginson," I repeated. "This is John's home."

"And what of the cause? What of the fight that has been and is to come?"

"I don't know," I said. "I don't know because I am not a fighter and I am not burying a cause. I am burying my husband—here. Here in North Elba. Here with the mountains. It was his wish—and it is mine."

Dawn.

Dressing quickly. Two sweaters.

"Two sweaters for everyone," I said to the girls. "And hats and coats."

Helping Ellen to dress. Stitching her wool leggings. Combing her hair. Finding her gloves.

Going to the privy. Feeling sick. Nauseous. Throwing up. Putting another cloth tight up between my legs. Feeling dizzy. Weak. Holding onto the door for a moment. Annie taking me back. Walking with Annie back to the house, to the grave, to the coffin. Each step blurring into the next. Merging into each other the way days do. And then the years. Each step, like each year, bringing me closer to John and further away.

The neighbors coming. I think all the neighbors came. Even those that had held back from us before. Those that had looked at us unevenly. Those that had whispered and shook their heads.

"Poor Browns," some had said. "Good neighbors, but crazy Abolitionists. Living as if they were fighting. Fighting when there was no need, when there was no war."

"Posterity will owe everlasting thanks to John Brown for he has attacked slavery with the weapons precisely adapted to bring it to the death," it was written.

Neighbors spreading out in front of the house like a fan. Coming into the house. One by one. Two by two. To pass by the coffin. To murmur. To say they were sorry. To say he was right. To say he was good. To say he was brave. To bow their heads and say nothing. To bow their heads and close their eyes.

And, of course, Ruth and Henry came, with their children. Ruth staring at the coffin. Touching the head of it.

"Grandfather Brown," she said to her son, J.J., "is blessed because he blessed others. And Grandfather Brown is at rest now, in Heaven."

Crying silently, her shoulders shaking, she came to me.

"My daughter. My first daughter..." I whispered.

"Mother," she said. "Mother," she said again.

And the Thompsons came. The parents of William and Dauphin. And the widows of William and Dauphin. William and Dauphin tossed into the ground as if they weren't fashioned in God's image. As if there wasn't a God. As if there wasn't a God who could see into a man's heart—even in Harper's Ferry.

"Don't take my life. I am a prisoner," William said.

But a shower of shots fell upon him and he tumbled into the river, and still the shots came. Alive for some hours, maybe four or five, clinging to a pier.

"I came only to free the slaves," Dauphin said.

And then a bayonet cut him through to silence. Soldiers dragging him onto the lawn in front of the engine house. A farmer spitting tobacco juice at his wounds.

Men coming to see the corpse. Women saying, "Let us see. We want to see, too."

The Thompsons coming slowly up the hill. Wagon wheels striking the frozen ground as if it was stone. Henry going to help them. Helping his parents. Helping his sisters-in-law. A carriage filled with the black of mourning.

"How much longer the volcano will smoke before the lava pours down, God alone knows. But one thing is certain—slavery or freedom must die in this struggle," it was written.

Facing the rock not far from the house.

"I want to be buried in the shadow of the rock," John had said.

Facing the tombstone leaning against the edge of the house. His grandfather's tombstone, reading, *John Brown, Who Died*

In New York, Sept. 3, 1776, In The 48th Year Of His Age.

And the inscriptions that would soon be added, just simple, the way John said they should be.

John Brown, Born May 9, 1800, was executed at Charlestown, Va., Dec. 2, 1859.

Oliver Brown, Born March 9, 1839, was killed at Harper's Ferry Oct. 17, 1859.

An old granite tombstone and not very large, so the back of it would also be used.

In Memory Of Frederick, Son Of John And Dianthe Brown, Born Dec. 21, 1830, And Murdered At Osawatomie, Kansas, Aug. 30, 1856, For His Adherence To The Cause Of Freedom.

Watson Brown, Born Oct. 7, 1835, Was Wounded At Harper's Ferry Oct. 17 And Died Oct. 19, 1859.

Turning from the tombstone. Facing the hole in the ground. Dug into the frozen winter ground. A wind blowing over it. Loose stalks of grass skipping here and there in the wind. Coming to rest by the rock.

"True, the slave is still there. So, when the tempest uproots a pine on our hills, it looks green for months—a year or two. Still, it is timber, not a tree. Thus has John Brown loosened the roots of the slave system," it was written.

John. Almost as if he was sleeping. A flush on his face. As if he had just come in from the barn. Or just rode home from town with the latest news or with his latest plan. Natural. That was the word. Except for the red scar around his neck, he looked so natural.

"Everyone is here," Mr. Phillips said. "Quite a good number. And, of course, more, so many more are in their own churches, in their own homes, looking into their own hearts. All people in proportion to their sensibility and self-respect sympathize with John Brown."

"Yes, I can see the people," I said. "Everyone is here and the time, I suppose, is here too."

Salmon closing the coffin. The lid slipping from his hand. Henry coming forward, helping to straighten the lid. And our black neighbor, Lyman Epps and his son helping to lift the coffin. Lifting the coffin. Carrying the coffin to the rock. To the hole in the ground.

Following. Hard to stand upright. Leaning on each other. First Annie, then Salmon. Then Ruth. J.J. leaving her side, coming to me, holding onto my skirt, lifting up his hands.

"Grandmother, I'm cold," he said.

Picking him up. Putting his hands inside my coat.

And Martha—so big with child, looking even bigger in the winter sun, so big her coat couldn't close over her bigness. Martha and Belle holding hands and holding Fred as if they were sharing him. Crying. Was it Belle who started crying or Fred? Then Ellen. Abbie wiping Ellen's eyes, her nose. Abbie carrying Ellen. Sarah standing close to the coffin, opening and closing the Bible that John had given her, trying to peek through the edge where the lid was not tight.

"He will not be buried. He will be planted and will spring up a hundred-fold," it was written.

And then Lyman Epps, turned to face the people.

"There was many a day—and night too—when John Brown sang this hymn. When we sang it together. When we saw the storm coming. When we knew the storm was here."

Then he turned his back to the people. He faced the coffin.

"And John, the storm is still here. Raging. And we are here. And one last time we will sing together."

His children came to join him. Their voices mingling with the wind. Singing:

Blow ye the trumpet blow,
the gladly solemn sound,
let all the nations know,
to earth's remotest bound.
The year of Jubilee has come,
return, ye ransom'd sinners, home.

Extol the Lamb of God,
the all-atoning Lamb,
redemption by his blood,
through all the world proclaim.

The year of Jubilee has come,
return, ye ransomed sinners, home.

The men—Salmon, Henry, Lyman and his son, lifting the coffin again. Lowering the coffin into the grave. Into the ground. The coffin bumping into the ground. Disappearing.

"John Brown has gone to join the company of the just made perfect," it was written.

Calling out in my head, "John, the waiting is over. Everyone is here. Everyone has come. Your friends are here. Your neighbors are here. Your family is here. Salmon is here." Gathering strength, continuing, "Johnny and Jase would have been here but they are so far away. And the grandchildren. They are here too."

Closing my eyes. Getting out of my head.

"John Brown is THE man of the nineteenth century. When he stretched forth his arm, the sky was cleared," it was written.

The Reverend Young—his voice, the words, "I have fought a good fight. I have finished my course. I have kept the faith. Henceforth there is laid up for me a crown of righteousness, which the Lord, the Judge shall give me..."

And the wind blew and the sun was stretching shadows.

And we stopped crying.

And we were widows.

And I went to change the pad between my legs.

CHAPTER 28

THOSE FIRST FEW DAYS, WINTER CAME EARLY... But no, winter did not come early. There, in that place both beautiful and hard, winter came as it always did. The fierce cold, the chilling wind, the driving rain, the snow—heaps of snow. All of it resting on the grave. John's grave mounding the snow, so that it looked like a tunnel.

Those first few days... The grave—like a new baby, like a big problem, like something that had to be done. Yes, that was it—like something that had to be done when there was nothing to do.

Ellen pulling on her boots.

"Are you going to look after the cat?" I asked.

"No, I have to fix something," she said.

Her coat and hat and gloves. Dragging the shovel. Dropping the shovel because it was too big. Crawling on her hands and knees, sinking into the snow, trying to brush the snow from the grave.

"Ellen, there's too much snow and it keeps on coming," I said, going after her, standing her up, closing her coat. "And if you catch a cold, who is that going to help, do you think?"

She looked at me. Was she going to cry?

"And don't cry because tears will just freeze to your face and peel away your skin. And who is that going to help?"

I took her hand, leading her from the grave, past the old tombstone, to the house.

It was winter—and what could you do with a grave?

She sat by the fire, drying her clothes, drinking a cup of warm milk sweetened with honey.

"Do you feel better?" I asked.

"Yes," she said. And then, "I want to draw a flower for father. A beautiful flower..."

Taking a sheet of newspaper and a piece of charcoal. The charcoal stroking the paper into a stalk and roots and a flower.

Sarah finishing her mending. Looking at Ellen. "A black flower?" she asked. Stopping. Pointing her finger at the picture. "There's no such thing as a black flower. Just like there's no black rain and no black sunshine."

Ellen thought for a minute.

"It's not black, it's gray," she said. "It's a gray flower, like the one that was in Ruth's yard. Remember that one?"

"That wasn't gray. It was yellow..."

Annie coming in from the barn.

"Look what I found," she said, holding up Sarah's Bible. "Sarah, how did your Bible get out in the snow?"

Sarah's face reddening.

"I put it there, on father's grave. I wanted it to be close to him. Don't you think it would please him..."

Sarah was pulling on her braid. Twisting it.

"But father wanted you to have it," Annie said. "He wanted you to keep it. He didn't want it to get blown apart or rained on or buried in the snow. If you want to please father..."

Then Annie looked down and saw Ellen. She was still drawing. Another black leaf on her flower.

"A black flower?" Annie asked.

"Black flowers..." Sarah began.

Black. Yes, a black flower. Black. Black. Black. Suddenly everything seemed dark. Too dark. Too dark and black.

"Black flowers. Black flowers. Is that all the thinking there is?" My voice was trembling and I could feel the anger rising up, spilling out, flowing out of me. Flowing

away from me, flowing far enough away to be gone.

"There is some cranberry dye in the upper cupboard, in the back..."

"Red flowers," Ellen said, clapping her hands, the way she did when she was surprised or happy. "Then I can have red flowers. Wouldn't father like red flowers for Christmas?"

Thinking... What would John say? He would say decoration was idle work, really no work at all. He would say, Better the music of the broom...

But I couldn't say that. "Yes," I said, "father would like red flowers for Christmas."

So Sarah took flour and water and made a paste. Annie went out to get some twigs. Ellen was drawing and coloring with red dye. And singing. Well, if not exactly singing, she was humming. Then Annie came back and was helping to cut out the flowers. Sarah was pasting the flowers together and then pasting them to the twigs and I was tying them with string for good measure.

Then we were ready. All of us—Ellen, Sarah, Annie, even Belle and Martha and Abbie—going to the grave. Opening John's Bible, reading from it:

"For I know nothing by myself; yet am I not hereby justified; but He that judgeth me is the Lord. Therefore judge nothing before the time, until the Lord come, who both will bring to light the hidden things of darkness, and will make manifest the counsels of the hearts: and then shall every man have praise of God."

And all of us, each one, planting a flower, a red flower in the snow, all around the grave. The grave looking as if it had a border, as if it was a blanket with an edging. The grave looking softer. Looking warmer.

Those were the first few days. That's the way they were. And then there were

the other days. The days that followed when we did not want to look at the grave. The nights when we did not want to dream. The days and nights we had to live through. Just that. Just doing all the things that had to be done.

Milk the cow. Get the chickens into the coop. Clean the barn. Fix the shelter for the sheep.Have the wood split and brought to the house. Make the house warm.

But there was time, other time, there must have been other time because Annie found the time to write a poem:

My sister can straddle and ride a horse

And she has the will to jump, of course.

Sit tall and straight, sit low and jump
Then look to the rear and there's the bump.

But looking back is never the best
Because looking forward is always the test.

So look you forward and don't be scared
And look to Heaven where love is shared.

Annie looking at us.

"Is it me?" Sarah asked. "Am I the sister in the poem? But I'm not scared. Do you think I'm scared?" she asked, without waiting for an answer. "Why do you think I'm scared?"

Annie holding the poem, the poem shaking in her hand. "It's not only you who shouldn't be scared. It's all of us."

We were quiet. Listening. Hearing the click of Martha's knitting needles. Belle's little Fred gulping and burping, a smile spreading across his face as if it belonged there. Looking at him. Sometimes seeing Watson. Sometimes seeing Oliver. And sometimes seeing Frederick. My Frederick. Hearing him cry. Then seeing him, buried in a grave so far away. Alone on the prairie. He was always afraid of being alone.

And thinking of Owen. Escaping. Climbing into the mountains. Hiding in laurel thickets. Hands bleeding. Feet swollen. Stomach empty. Where was he now? Was he able to find his way north? Was he able to find help, to find friends? Was he able to rest? Was he able to sleep and go on?

"About six feet in height," the Richmond paper said, "fair complexion, though

somewhat freckled, with red hair and very heavy whiskers of the same color. He is a spare man, with regular features, and deep blue eyes. And there is a $500 reward for his capture."

Coming back from that world to this one, from those children to these children.

"And don't be scared," Annie was saying, as if she was talking to herself.

"Is that all?" Sarah asked. "Is that the way the poem ends?"

"Yes, that's the way the poem ends. Don't be scared. Just don't be scared."

"Trusting in God," I said, "in His love and wisdom."

Trying. We were all trying. Trying to face today and tomorrow without being scared. Trying to face the shadows that came out of nowhere, that grew strangely and suddenly.

But if we weren't scared, we were worried—how we could fill our days and nights with our lives. How we could fill our hands with work. How we could live—hold up our heads and not look back. Or look back just a little—without being punished.

"Dear Mr. Stearns," I wrote when I was sick. "The girls still have some of the money from berry picking and Martha has the five sheep that Oliver left to her, but we don't have that much to put toward meeting our tax bill. It is $10. We thought we would be able to meet this bill, but had to lend the money to a black woman, much poorer than we. So I am forced to ask if you have received any of the money that has been promised us?"

"Dear Mr. Stearns," I wrote when Ellen was sick. "We are trying to get through the winter as best we can. We need money for a hired hand. I don't see how we can get along without one. Also, I would like to buy some sheep. That way we can be more independent."

"Dear Mr. Bullard," I wrote when Annie was sick. "I received your offer to educate my three youngest children. I hardly know how to make suitable expression of gratitude to friends for offers so sympathizing, comforting, and benevolent. So I thank you, but I have already made arrangements to send my girls to school in Concord, Massachusetts. May you find ample reward in a reliance upon the promises of Him who is a Father to the fatherless and the widows."

"Dear Mr. Sanborn," I wrote when Sarah and Ellen were sick. "Thank you for admitting Annie and Sarah to your school. May the Lord God of orphans and widows repay you."

"Dear Mr. Stearns," I wrote when Fred and Belle and Abbie were sick. "I have been in hopes of receiving some help from the Haitian fund before this time as I want to use some of it to buy sheep and to get a horse and wagon which we need very much."

"Dear Mr. Redpath," I wrote when I was sick again and Abbie still was not well. "Has your book about my husband been published? Any money which you receive from it and decide to give us, as you said you wanted to do, would be greatly appreciated. We need to get the house plastered. It's been so cold."

"Dear Frances Ellen Watkins," I wrote when Martha, who had been taking care of everyone, one after the other in their sicknesses, thought that her time was close at hand. "Thank you for the sum of $54 that you have collected for us. My husband's faith in the people of color has proved beyond a doubt to be correct."

And then it was a new year and our thoughts turned from money to Martha. It was her time.

Henry clambered up the hill in his wagon bringing wood panels for a partition.

"Don't cloud your mind for a minute," he said, working quickly. "Before the pains come hard, you'll have your own little room."

The rest of us pasting the newspapers we had saved, pasting them up and down the walls, upside down and sideways so Martha couldn't see the news, so the news was no longer the news, so the news was just a blur of black and white. Trying to keep the snow from flurrying in. The snow sometimes landing on her bed cover.

"Push. And then rest. Push. And then rest. Try to breathe deeply. Try to relax. You must. You must. Think of your baby. Think of Oliver..."

Her legs pulled up. Her gown cold with her sweating. The hair between her legs matted. Her breathing so quick, her breath squeaking in and out of her. Her voice—as if it came from a distance far away, from another place.

"Oh, Mother Brown, I feel it. I feel it. It's coming. The baby, my baby is coming. My son is coming. Oh, Oliver... Oh, Oliver... My dearest love..."

Resting. Trying to smile. Drinking some sage tea. Annie riding for the midwife.

Pushing again. Pushing. Hour after hour. Sarah keeping the fire up. Ellen bringing the towels.

"Is she dying?" Ellen asked, her forehead wrinkled, almost as if she was an old woman.

"No, she's not dying," I said. "You should know that hard things don't have to mean dying. Hard things can mean living too."

Annie and the midwife returning.

"Snow and ice held us up some," Annie said.

"Are there pains? How often?" the midwife asked, uncorking a small bottle of

brandy.

Martha shaking her head. "No, nothing to drink," she said. "I never have... No spirits."

"Is she dying?" Ellen asked again.

"No, she's not dying," the midwife said. "She's just doing the work women do since the sinning of Eve in the garden."

Pushing. Pushing life into this world. Pulling it from somewhere else. Pushing it...

"It's coming. Isn't it coming? It must be coming."

The head. Seeing the dark ball. Seeing the shoulders and chest and arms. Then the legs. The baby–thirteen babies, and I had forgotten how tiny they were.

Cutting the cord.

"Here she is," I said, cleaning the baby, drying her, wrapping her in a blanket.

"She?" Martha asked. "Are you sure? She?" she repeated. "Are you sure? A daughter..." Turning to the baby. Gathering her into her arms. "A daughter. I have a daughter..."

"Not too big. It's likely she weighs about five pounds," the midwife said.

"I wanted a son," Martha said. "I wanted a son for Oliver."

Holding little Olive one day, two days. Holding her. Then slowly watching her eyes close. Trying to open her eyes. To keep them open. Watching her body shake. Watching her body turn blotchy and red.

"Is it because I wanted a son? Mother Brown, am I being punished? Is it because I said it would be a son?"

"The Lord's way is the Lord's way. His will is His will..." I did not finish. What could I say? Yes, you are being punished... No, you are not being punished...

Putting her breast to the baby's mouth. Opening her mouth with her finger. Stroking her throat. Holding the mixture of mullein and syrup.

Saying, "Swallow. Swallow."

Crying, "Swallow. Swallow."

Listening to the baby. Listening to Olive... her cries weaker and weaker.

"She will be a pure shining light in Heaven," the preacher said.

The emptiness that came into our house then. As if death could pull the walls of the house down on you, keeping the sickness there–in your house, in your head, in your heart. As if death could make your house a grave.

The worry within the four walls of the house and the worry beyond it. The worry and the scare.

Martha turning her head from side to side, turning her hand from this to that. Doing nothing and wanting nothing.

"You have to eat," Annie said, bringing soup, bringing stew, bringing bread and butter. "You are a sister to me. You must be strong."

Martha so weak. Confused. Whispering.

"There is no reason. I have given my all. There is nothing more to live for. There is nothing more to give."

Bleeding. Being weak and bleeding.

"Is she dying?" Ellen asked.

This time no one answered. There was no need to answer.

"She is dying," Ellen said, beginning to cry. Then stopping. "Can angels fly over mountains?" she asked.

"Yes," I said, as if I knew something about angels. "Angels can fly over mountains."

Coughing. Clutching the sides of the bed. Closing her eyes.

"It's more than likely she got up too early," the midwife said.

"I see her. I think I can see her," Ellen said, going to the window, her face pressed against the window. Looking out.

"She has gone to join her family in the family of the Lord," the preacher said.

CHAPTER 29

THE LIFE THAT HAD TO COME. The living and the dying. The war that had to come. The war that took everyone into it. The war that didn't let go.

Her name was Mary Todd, before she was caught in the middle of the war, before she was trapped in it. Before she was torn apart. Before she became Mary Todd Lincoln.

"Look at me. Look at me," she said.

"Listen to me. Listen to me," she said.

"Let me read. Let me know. Let me talk. Let me choose," she said.

"I will marry that lanky man because I love him," she said, "because his heart is as long as his arms and because he will be President one day."

"I have chosen Abraham Lincoln because I have chosen love," she said. "And love is the miracle that survives. It is the miracle that grows strong. It is the miracle that lives forever."

Miracles.

A young woman talking about miracles. The miracle of love. The miracle of life. Thinking she could make room in the world for herself. For her husband. For her family. Thinking she could raise her sons. Thinking they could grow into their names and into their lives. Thinking and not thinking. Not thinking because everything that happens does not always seem possible.

And also thinking. Thinking she could make a miracle happen, as if she could know. As if she could do, like planning a party or preparing a feast. Thinking she could know which friends would turn against her. Thinking, if she thought about it at all, that she could choose her enemies.

Mary Todd. Lively, lovely, witty and loving. Before the south called her a traitor and the north called her a spy. Before her husband was shot as he sat next to her, blood from his wound seeping into her gown, spreading out like a monster with a hundred hands. And before Robert, her first child and now her only child, told a judge and jury, "There is no doubt. My mother is insane."

"Let me have a flower for my hair," she said.

"Let me have a bow for my dress," she said.

"Let me dance in the garden," she said.

"Let me sing in the nursery," she said.

But there was a war. The war that had to come. The war that was supposed to last a week or a month or three months. The war that would only last a year. The war that ran away with itself. The war that found numbers. One number for every body. One number for the wounds of that body. One number for the death, quick or slow, of that body. The war that found the numbers it needed and killed them. Numbers giving up on themselves, caving in on themselves. Who could count the numbers in five acres of bodies?

And in the beginning there were people on horseback, in carriages and wagons.

"Let's follow the soldiers and see the show," the men said, carrying revolvers and rifles and hoping to shoot something.

"Let's bring hampers of food and chests of wine," the women said, carrying opera glasses and hoping to see something.

The war.

Finally the war.

When the war came...

"Yes," Harriet Tubman said. "If you want me to read from the Bible, I will. If you want me to blow a trumpet, I will. If you want me to lead my people to the cause, to tell them to burn houses and barns and railroads and bridges, I will."

The war that was a miracle. The war that came from John's life and from his grave. And from Oliver's grave, buried without a coffin on the banks of the Shenandoah. Buried with Dangerfield Newby, who thought he could keep his wife and children from the slavedealer's pen. Buried face to face, their arms around each other. "A nigger and a rat," it was said. And Watson... Poor Watson—there was no grave, no marker, no body.

"When the war is over we can live in Springfield," she said.

"When the war is over we will travel in Europe," she said.

"When the war is over I will wear a white dress and you, your black suit—more handsome than ever," she said.

"When the war is over we will have more friends than enemies," she said.

"When the war is over and the grieving is over, there will be love," she said.

Soldiers marching through Washington ton their way to Virginia, to the Battle of Bull Run. to the Battle of Balls' Bluff, to the Battle of Fredericksburg, to the Battle of Richmond.

Soldiers marching smartly, saluting the President and Mrs. Lincoln. Soldiers singing the Battle Hymn of the Republic. Soldiers singing about John–

John Brown's body lies a mouldrin in the grave
His truth goes marching on...

Weeping when I first heard it. Weeping each and every time I heard it, but after a while the tears not showing themselves. And with the tears, at the same time, my heart was beating a little faster and I held my head up a little higher. And sometimes I was breathless, like a young girl racing up a hill. Like an old woman...

And after the Emancipation Proclamation, black soldiers marched.

"Could we die in a more noble cause?" Osborn Anderson asked.

"Could we die for a cause which would induce men more to honor us and the angels more readily to receive us in the home of everlasting joy?" Frances Merriam asked.

Asking and answering.

"This is my war," they said.

"This is our war," they said.

"I'm answering with my feet," William Copeland said,

"because my brother was with John Brown and was hanged with him. I'm answering with my feet and I'm carrying a gun."

Numbers. How the numbers grew. A mountain of numbers.

Then a note from Johnny.

"I am returning to Kansas to fight," he said. "No matter what else is said, this is the war that will end slavery."

Salmon agreeing.

"This is the beginning and the end is in sight," he said.

Abbie nursing Minnie. Johanna sitting at Salmon's feet, pulling on the laces of his boots.

"It's death," Abbie said, her cheeks flushing red, her eyes blinking, as they did when she was excited or angry. It's death and dying all over again. She turned to me. "Mother Brown, tell him not to do it. Tell him you have had enough. Tell him the Browns have done enough."

"Enough?" Salmon asked. "In the teeth of evil, in the throat and belly and heart of evil—you say enough? What is enough?"

Quiet. Just the baby sucking, then spitting and coughing. Abbie holding her up over her shoulder.

"If we have waited for this war, if we welcome it, can we turn our backs to it?"

The quiet flowing in around me as I spoke.

"Can we?" I asked again. "Can we turn our backs to the day of Jubilee?"

"Not our backs. Just our men..." Abbie said, biting her lip.

"It's what has to be done," Salmon said, "and I have already mustered a regiment of forty men."

He stood up, tall and straight. Then he bent down, swinging Johanna to his shoulders.

"Daddy, daddy," she said, "swing me higher."

Johanna swinging back and forth.

"As high as this?" Salmon asked.

She laughed. She giggled. Her hair bouncing around her.

"Higher. Higher," she said.

Not afraid. Just being happy and giggling. Just that. Like a child. But I didn't remember my children giggling. I don't think they ever did.

Salmon put Johanna down.

"Sometimes I think of Watson and Oliver," he said.

"Yes?" Abbie asked.

"That's all. Sometimes I just think about them."

I took the baby from Abbie and rocked her in my arms. I smiled at her and she smiled at me. Then I looked past her smile, past her blue eyes, her wispy hair, yellow as the yellow birds that I remembered and the leaves that were falling everywhere.

Thinking of my babies. Thinking of my sons. The ones that fought. The ones that couldn't fight again.

"I'm not for killing," Jase wrote. "I am planting grapes and fruit trees and I am trying to build a flying machine."

"I can't do it," Owen wrote. "My arm is weaker, my eyes are less steady and I am tired from morning till night."

It was two o'clock and bells were tolling. Six gray horses took the casket down Pennsylvania Avenue to the Capitol.

The preacher said, "Yield to the behest of God and drink this cup of submission. God of the just, we yield to Thy behest and drink it up."

A Negro regiment was the first to file past the coffin. Then dignitaries and citizens. And mourners. Negro mourners. Some clutching a Bible. Some crying, "The Messiah is dead."

And Mary Todd Lincoln? Where was she? She was hiding. For the rest of her life she was hiding. With headaches. With weakness. With pain. Hiding in her room. Hiding in her bed. Hiding in shadows. Seeing her children there sometimes. Seeing her husband there sometimes. Hiding but also traveling—or escaping—to find herself or to lose herself. Traveling and buying clothes. A new dress and another new dress. Putting them in boxes. So many boxes. Was she crazy? Was it a woman's craziness? The craziness of a woman who loved. The craziness of a woman who chose.

Choosing.

"Choose life," the Bible says, "that you may live.

Learning that there are choices. Learning to choose.

"Yes," I said, "we will go to California."

CHAPTER 30

Was it easy?

"We have blessings," Abbie said. "I know we do, but this place is like a hole in the woods. And it's lonesome. A lonesome hole in the woods."

"With six months of winter," Annie said.

"And the other six months are almost as cold," Sarah added.

Sun.

Sun and softness. They seemed to go together. Sun and the morning. Sun for the meadow and garden. Sun for the clothesline. Sun for the house. Remembering dust motes dangling in the sun. A baby reaching for them. Scattering them.

"A long time ago people worshipped the sun," Abbie said.

"Because they had it or because they didn't have it?" Sarah asked.

"Because they knew they needed it," Annie said.

Sun.

Sun for the road and for walking–slowly, and for looking. Sun for the forest, its shadows changing sharp angles into something else.

"I want to change the angles into something more beautiful," Sarah said, learning to paint, painting the sun into her pictures.

Sun.

Sun just for shining.

The sun shining in California. "The land of golden opportunities," everyone said.

Was it easy?

The packing. The leaving. The going.

"And father's grave?" Ellen asked. "Who will watch it?"

"Ellen, it's hard for me, too," I wanted to say, but she turned away and I shrugged.

Going to the grave after we were packed, when we were ready to leave. The summer coming to a close. Days starting to shorten. Going alone. Walking the well worn path. "Blow ye the trumpets blow..." those words racing through my head. Bending to pull on a sticker vine that was growing at the foot of the grave.

"It's too hard, John," I said. "It's too poor—for the animals, for the people. It's too cold. It's too lonely."

My heart beating so quickly, as if I had just come up the hill from the creek. I took a deep breath.

"The slaves are free and we are going to California," I said.

Looking down, seeing blood on my finger. Holding my hand over the grave, waiting until one drop of blood had fallen. Then two. My blood falling on John's stone. A pink spot. Two pink spots.

So hard to breathe. Breath escaping from me. Rushing from me—from my mouth, from my heart—to the stone. I could see it. I thought I could see it. And then a tear.

"The slaves are free and we are going to California," I said again.

CHAPTER 31

IT WAS A PEACEFUL NIGHT. The sky was so big. The stars were so bright, so white and clear. And it was quiet—only the murmur of voices, and the pots and pans and kettles. The crackling of campfires.

Last night it was different.

Zena had come out of her wagon shouting, "I hear it. I hear it. Don't you hear it? Those are wolves howling," she said. "You better watch out for your livestock and your children. They don't care if they get one or the other."

Her husband was cleaning his rifle. He put it down, turned her around and pushed her back toward the wagon.

"I know a wolf when I hear one," she called over her shoulder. "My baby was carried off by a wolf, and when you put your head in the sand, you get more than sand in your face."

Just then Ellen was coming from Salmon's wagon bringing the beef sausage and potatoes. "When? When was your baby eaten by a wolf?" she asked.

"I didn't say eaten, young lady. I said carried off..."

"When was your baby carried off?" Ellen began again. "When did it happen? In the morning or in the night? Before we crossed the river? Here on the trail? Did you ever find it? Was it dead? It was dead, wasn't it?"

I knew it was Ellen's dream. Being carried off. Not a wolf, but a black bird fastening onto her braids. A dream of fear. That she would be hurt. That she would be dropped. That she would be lost. Dangling. Alone. Starting when John died, the dream, the fear, the crying out in the night. But Zena didn't know that—and she had her own fears. Her own pain.

"Ellen," I said, perhaps more sharply than I needed to get her attention. "Where are the apples? Did you forget them?" And when she turned from Zena, I said, "It's not right to talk like that. No one has a right to bring back what's full of pain. No one has a right to bring back what is best forgotten."

Minnie started to cry. Abbie called from the wagon door, "It's too noisy out there. The babies can't sleep."

"It's not my fault it's noisy. It's the wolves..."

Then Mr. Woodruff came walking down the line of wagons, walking so fast and straight. Looking like a soldier, almost marching. Stopping when he came to Zena.

"Zena, calm down. It's alright," he said. "Eyes and ears are personal things. Everyone has their own. And I'm thinking that what you hear are coyotes. Wolves and coyotes are kin, you know, and they howl the same way."

Zena shrugged. "Maybe you know best, Mr. Woodruff, but if it's not wolves, the good Lord knows it might be Indians," she said, crossing herself. "Those savages come in the night like snakes."

"Snakes don't come in the night," Annie said.

"Are you sure?" Ellen asked.

"I'm sure," Annie answered.

"Are you sure?" Sarah asked.

"About snakes or Indians?"

"Both."

"I'm sure," Annie said. "Almost sure."

Listening.

I didn't hear wolves. I didn't hear coyotes. There was a whippoorwill. Maybe rabbits and gophers rustling in the brush. Mr. Woodruff returning to the head of the wagon train.

Ellen started to sneeze and cough.

"The wind is coming from the north and it's picking up," I said. "Put on a jacket and get the beds ready."

Ellen climbed into the wagon. Sarah poked up the fire. Annie and I went to milk the cows.

But that was last night, and now, this night, there was only the hoot of an owl—a call and an answer.

"That's a good sign, don't you agree?" Zena asked, coming

out of her wagon, catching her hem on the axle handle.

"Everything is a good sign as long as it doesn't snow before we get to California," Annie said. "Don't you agree with that?"

"I do. I do." Zena tugged her hem free. "Summer snow? Now that would be something, wouldn't it? We could have snowmen—or snowwomen, and put grass on their heads."

Zena laughing. Annie laughing. So good to see Annie laughing.

Yes, it was a peaceful night and we thought we were safe. Slowing down. Time slowing down. The time to bake a quick bread and spread it with the milk that was churned into butter as the wagon rolled back and forth, back and forth, all day. Eating slowly. Finishing. Stirring the new batch of pepper sauce with one hand, holding Minnie with the other, while Abbie helped Salmon with the sheep. Annie was writing to Belle. "We finally made it," she wrote, "crossing the Missouri River on the Ferry. There were more wagons than you can imagine, hundreds upon hundreds of wagons. It would have been easy to get separated but we just stayed in the middle, following Salmon's wagon in front, and George and Ezra keeping the wagon with Salmon's sheep close behind us. And now we have joined the regular train. So we are going. Really on our way. And we have long days for traveling—sometimes hot and sometimes cold, but sometimes also beautiful. Yesterday Abbie and I went over the hill into another ravine and got bunches of flowers. In a week or two I think the prairies will be like a flower garden. A big flower garden filled with June rose bushes."

"Tell her I miss her, too," Sarah said taking out her sketch pad and pencil. She started to sketch. "Tell her if my sketch turns out right, I'll send it to her."

Ellen finished brushing her hair and started to count the stars.

"There's a bright one," she said. "I'm going to make a wish." And she closed her eyes.

"Devil's work," John used to say. "Devil's work and Devil's play."

"Devil's work," I almost said. "You should pray, not wish..."

But maybe not, who could tell for sure? Because what was the difference between a child's prayer and her wish? And here, now, we were going to California, and wasn't that a prayer and a wish?

Abbie took Johanna and went to the river to wash the dishes. Annie closed her letter and joined her. Their voices drifting into the night. I thought of how far we had come. I thought of how far we still had to go. The rivers behind us and the rivers before us. The mountains. The graves we passed along the way. The little ones. Holding Minnie so tight in my arms. Pulling her blanket up around her shoulders. Putting on her warm pink hat, tying the ribbon beneath her chin. Putting a cloth of sage and sugar on her lip, the blister that wouldn't go away. Thinking that tomorrow I should cook a soup.

And then I was thrown back—how many years? 10? 11? 12?, it was before Ellen was born—and I was thinking of Cyrus.

"I'm going west," he had said, the way some folks said, "I'm going home," or "I'm going into town," or "I'm going to church."

I could see him sure and tight on his horse. Shaking hands with John, waving once, and then not looking back. Disappearing in the distance. Did he escape? Did he get to California? Did he find gold? A man as black as night, was he able to come out of hiding and stand in the sun? Was he rich? Did he know what happened to John at Harper's Ferry? Did he know what happened to Oliver and Watson...

The girls came back from the river.

"Johanna almost went swimming," Abbie said.

Sarah and Ellen began to dry the dishes. Abbie took Minnie into the wagon. Annie carried Johanna who was twisting and turning.

"Wriggling like a fish," Annie said. "No wonder you like the water so much." I started a letter to Owen. "I have been thinking of you, especially to thank you for being so kind to Sarah when she was visiting you and sickly. I was worried to death about scarlet fever but she seems to have escaped it. And so far, we thank the Lord for all good things as we have been well, even little Minnie, who is big enough to sit up by herself, when she gets out of the wagon. Mile after mile, one day lumbers into the next. We have been traveling so much, I don't know how we will ever get used to a solid floor and a solid roof, but that is a worry we look forward to. Salmon sends his wishes. I am hoping to hear from Ruth. Can you ask Henry if he got the Bibles for the grandchildren? Tell Johnny and Jase that I will write to them soon—maybe from California."

Abbie coming out of the wagon.

"The children are in bed and Johanna is counting as high as she can until she falls asleep," she said.

The fires dying down. Lanterns going out. Annie got the ligament oil. She shook the bottle. "I hope it lasts," she said, taking the cap off. And one after the other, we rubbed each other's necks and arms and backs.

"How many times we turned them this way. How many times we turned them that way. Around the stones. Around the mud. Trying to keep up. Whoa, faster. Trying to be careful. Whoa, slower," Annie said.

"Oxen are only oxen," I said, as I rubbed my right shoulder, then my left shoulder, feeling as if I was still tugging on the reins.

"And driving them is driving them, but California will be worth it," Sarah said.

"A hundred times, we turned a hundred times, but California will be worth it," Ellen agreed, "because we will live in a house and have a piano."

And then something changed. I'm not sure how it began, but I heard voices becoming loud and rough. Men's voices.

"Go back to Missouri."

"Go back to Ohio."

"Remove that flag or we'll do it for you."

And suddenly being safe was giving way to danger.

And again the voice, the fighting voice, "Mr. Woodruff, we don't aim to hurt anyone, but we're telling you to remove that Union flag or we'll do it for you."

People coming from their wagons. Gathering. Soon there were two sides.

"When you joined this train the Union flag was flying, and

as long as I'm here, when you leave this train the Union flag will still be flying. Old Glory, high and proud." Mr. Woodruff said.

Men moving in the night. Salmon joining them, standing next to Mr. Woodruff. Then, before we knew what was happening, Johanna slid out the flap at the back of the wagon and was running after Salmon, calling, "Papa. Papa. I want to go too."

Abbie running after Johanna. Bringing her back. Johanna crying, "I counted to a hundred and I'm big enough to go with Papa."

"Only sometimes," I said, wiping her tears as Abbie tied her to the wagon wheel. "And sometimes you're just big enough to stay right here with your mother and me."

Hearing the voices. Searching for Salmon, somewhere in the darkness. Finding him in the group of men. Looking so much like John. But taller, I thought. Yes, taller. Not less eager, but slower. More solid. His feet so firm to the ground.

Thinking I should call to him. Thinking I should tell him something. Thinking I should give him something. But he was a man, past any of my giving.

Watching—as a mother watches.

"You must follow the wisdom of the Great Mystery," another mother said.

Her name was Her Holy Door. Her son was Sitting Bull.

Watching as a mother watches, as she mixed the paint, coloring it—sometimes yellow, sometimes red. Green, when her son dreamed of the White Buffalo Woman and smoked her pipe. Black when there was a victory.

"You are a hunter," she said. "Give the calves that you kill to the poor who have no horses."

Watching for his return. Hoping. Praying. Waiting. Ready to make a feast. To eat. To listen to his stories. To laugh. Later, to cut the meat into thin slices and hang it in the sun to dry.

"You are a chief," she said. "You have sucked sweet grass and your mouth opens to the truth."

As a mother watches. As a mother turns her face from one

direction to another. Before each battle. After each battle. Battle after battle. Afraid he might not return.

"You are too old," she said. "You have wives and children. You must hang back in time of war. Let the younger men fight. They can make coup and bring back the horses and the scalps."

I moved closer. To see what was happening. To hear what was happening. "Go back to Tennessee," came from one side.

"Go back to the gallows at Harper's Ferry," came from the other side.

I saw Salmon starting to move toward the sound. Mr. Woodruff holding one arm. Zena's husband holding his other arm.

"We don't have to be the first to fight," Mr. Woodruff said. "We'll just make sure that we are the last."

What did Salmon say? I don't know. It was lost in the wind.

Moving closer, passing one wagon, two wagons. Feeling cold from the wind and the night, but my feet kept on going. My head kept on going. My heart was racing. I was talking to myself. "This isn't Kansas," I said. "This isn't Harper's Ferry. This time I am here. And whatever is going to happen, I will be here when it happens. I will stay here. I will face it. I will know it. Maybe I will help it."

Lanterns moving. People moving. Another woman coming closer. Then two. One woman carrying her baby.

"Be careful," she said, it seemed to no one in particular, just scattering her words into the group of men.

"It's only a flag," another woman said.

And another, "You're not soldiers."

"Soldiers?" Zena said, coming up beside me. "I have brothers soldiering on both sides of the war..."

"Get back," a deep voice said. "You're in the way."

But no one answered. No one said anything. Not the men or the women, and then almost as suddenly as it started, it stopped. The men and women following each other to their wagons. And where they had been there was nothing. Just space.

Walking back to our wagons. Hurrying to keep up with Salmon's long strides.

"Do you think they will come back? Do you think there will be trouble?" I asked.

"Mr. Woodruff is as tough as anybody and when he stands his ground the others will give way. Besides, they need him."

Salmon slowing his steps so I could catch up.

"Anyway," he said, "there's no need to worry because I'll be keeping a watch tonight. And after me it will be George and then Ezra."

"That's good," I said. "I know that's good." And then more quietly, "I know that's the way it is, but is there no end to hatred? Does it just go on and on? Were all the deaths for nothing?"

"Hatred has to run itself out, one way or the other," Salmon said, helping me into my wagon, and going to his.

Abbie was waiting for him.

"They know about us, don't they?" she asked.

Salmon nodded.

"And they'll be out to get us, won't they?"

Salmon stood his rifle by the wagon door and said nothing.

Then one day went by. One night. Two days. Two nights. Three days and nothing happened.

"And nothing is going to happen," Salmon said, "for one reason that there are more of us."

Even so, we were careful. After that there were no more long walks where you could stretch your legs or gather flowers or look for turtles or frogs. And when the girls went to wash the dishes, Salmon or George or Ezra went with them. Even Johanna stayed close to the wagon.

"It's nothing special. It's just another worry. That's all there is to it," I told Ellen. "And soon it will be over."

Walking quickly past some wagons. Not looking into someone's eyes. Not turning your back to someone. Sometimes startling to a loud noise or a strange one.

But that's not the reason we left the train. We didn't leave because we were frightened and we weren't looking for sport or adventure and we didn't know—we could be trading one danger for another, jumping from the frying pan into the fire.

"The reason we're leaving is to go north of the Platte River on the Oregon Trail," Salmon said. "That way when we get to California, we'll be closer to Uncle Hinckley and we can start right in to get settled."

Salmon wasn't asking and no one was answering because he sounded so sure, so matter of fact, as if it would really happen. As if God would grant us a new life.

Zena brought us a potato pudding. and a wide-brimmed bonnet for Ellen.

"Watch out for snakes and Indians," she called as we pulled out of line and turned away to the right. "And wolves. Don't forget the wolves."

Then it was just us.

"Just us and freedom and California," Annie said. "And sun."

CHAPTER 32

AND CLOUDS. AND RAIN. AND WIND. And dust. And long cold nights. Long cold darknesses.

And through it all, the wilderness. Always the wilderness. Day after day.

And sometimes, maybe in the heat of the day, when one stone or one bush shimmered and merged into the next, I wondered about the purpose of so much emptiness. The purpose of so much openness. So much distance. Was it a test only the strong could pass? A trial? Was I too old? Was I too tired?

Salmon's wagon slowed and stopped. We pulled alongside. He pointed to a large cottonwood tree.

"We'll camp here," he said.

Stopping. Once again an end to the bumping and the tossing from side to side, the shaking up and down.

"If the milk churns into butter, what will we churn into?" Ellen asked, wrinkling her forehead into her half laughing, half serious look.

"Maybe we will churn into butterflies or buttercups," Annie said.

"Maybe butterfingers. That's more likely," Sarah added.

"None of that is likely, so don't be teasing your sister. And if we churn or turn into anything," I said to Ellen, "we'll turn into Californians and live in a house with a piano and you will learn to play songs and hymns and marches."

Ellen smiled. "Annie will teach and make money. Sarah will draw. And I will play and sing."

"All of us will sing. You and me and Sarah and you too,

Mama," Annie said. "Do you know that I have never heard you sing?" She didn't wait for me to answer. "But in California, we are going to sing. They will call us The Singing Browns."

Stopping. Good to stop and to stop staring into the distance–to the front where we were going, to the back where someone might be coming after us. Good to talk–not shouting over the creaks and the rumbles.

"The wagons are okay," Salmon said, checking the hitches and the wheels. "And George and Ezra are letting the sheep out to graze. So do you think a fisherman has time to catch dinner?"

"There's always time for that," Abbie said. "And we'll have the fry pot ready."

"Me too. Me too," Johanna insisted, jumping up and down, holding onto Salmon's legs.

Salmon nodded. He took her hand.

"No two ways about it," he said, "every fisherman needs a partner."

Abbie shifting Minnie in her arms.

"Watch out for snakes," she called after them.

Sitting around a blanket under a tree. Just sitting. The dishes around us. The food around us. For a minute or two just sitting.

"This is like a picnic," Annie said. "A real picnic. Look, we even have ants."

I cut up the potatoes. Stirred the pot. The smell of rabbit stewing with the wild onion we found yesterday.

"Can we roast the apples tonight?" Ellen asked.

"I think we might just do that. Why not? We have the apples and the time. And we'll roast them with hickory nuts."

"We used to have picnics once a year, for Easter," Abbie said. "I guess people living on the land are too busy clearing it and working it to picnic on it."

"And it was always too cold. Don't you remember?" Annie asked.

Salmon and Johanna returning.

"No snakes, but no fish either," he said. "Will you take us back empty-handed? I'm hungrier than a hound dog."

George and Ezra coming back.

"I am a hound dog," George said. "Just ask the sheep."

"Me too. Me too," Ezra said, jumping up and down. "I'm a little Johanna hound dog, you can tell by the way I'm jumping."

Joking. Talking. Eating. Resting. Looking at the sky. Clouds coming from the west. At first white, then turning gray. Little spiders climbing up and down the tree on invisible threads.

"Indians eat willow buds," Annie said. "When I was a teacher at the Freedman's School in Virginia, the other teacher was part Negro and part Indian and she said that's what some Indians do."

Abbie coming back from milking the cows.

"The forage hasn't been too good the last few days and Bessie might be drying up," she said.

Sarah broke a branch from the tree. Waved it. The white fluff floating in the air. Settling on heads and shoulders.

"Maybe cottonwoods have buds that we can eat," she said.

Ellen undid her hair and began to twist it around her finger. She was excited. "We could be like Indians. We could. We could dress like Indians and eat like Indians."

"But you have forgotten something," I said. "If we were Indians, how would we pray?"

"We would pray the same as always because we wouldn't be real Indians. We would just pretend to be Indians."

Sarah got her pencils and sketch pad.

"I think I'll sketch this tree. I'll call it the Stopping Tree by the Platte River," she said, walking close to the tree. Touching it.

Feeling good. Even the soreness and the tiredness feeling good. Feeling whole. Everything in place. Everyone in place. Feeling strong. As if we could really do this. As if we would...

"This is my first picnic," I said, leaning back on one elbow and looking up at the tree. Into the tree. Its big sweep. Looking past the lower branches. Following the branches inward to the trunk. Past a little nest, an old nest. Twigs hanging out the side. Looking higher. Squinting. Turning my head. Seeing something strange. Something smooth and tan. What was it? Staring... Staring until I could make out what it was.

"Who would have thought," I said. "Who would have thought," I repeated louder.

"What?" Annie asked. "Who would have thought what?"

"A blanket in a tree... Who would put a blanket high up in a tree?"

But then, still looking, I saw it was more than a blanket. I saw hair. I saw hair braided with some kind of fur. That's what it looked like. Hair and fur hanging down the side of a dark face. A reddish face.

"Who would have thought," I said again. "Look! There! There's an Indian in that blanket. There's a dead Indian right above our heads."

Salmon jumped up, reaching for his rifle.

"George, Ezra," he called. "Take cover. Watch the sheep."

"Are we surrounded?" Ellen asked.

"No," I answered. I took a deep breath, trying to keep calm. "We are not surrounded. It's just one Indian..."

Ellen dropped her bowl, burned her fingers and started to cry.

"Now what harm is there in one dead Indian?" I asked, pressing a cloth into butter and greasing her hands.

Sarah stood up. She walked close to the blanket. She peered up into the tree.

"Should we give him a proper burial?" she asked.

"Maybe this is a proper burial," Annie said. "Maybe his tribe thinks the tree will protect him—or that the tree will protect his spirit. Maybe his tribe worships trees."

Ellen stopped crying.

"Why can't they use a grave?" she asked. "Why can't they dig a hole in the ground like everyone else?" She almost shuddered. "I take back everything I said about wanting to be like an Indian. I don't want to be dead in a tree. And then the birds might come..."

"Or vultures," Abbie said, shielding Minnie in her arms and holding Johanna tight in front of her.

"Well, I guess we won't be camping here after all," Salmon said. "There's no need to camp in a graveyard. We'll just move on down the trail."

"Hurry," Ellen said. "We have to hurry."

Hitching up the animals. Getting the sheep back into the

wagon. Getting ourselves back into the wagons. Traveling down the trail. Just a little ways. The sun beginning to set. A vast sunset. Pink and orange. Once again slowing down. Stopping. And then, turning around, seeing the dust of wagons in the distance. Coming closer. The dust. The wagons.

"Don't worry, that's not the dust of Indians," Salmon said, but he and George and Ezra stood in front of the wagons with their rifles. "Indians don't travel in covered wagons, but there's no need to take chances," he said quietly, so quietly it was almost a whisper. Annie, Sarah, Ellen and me coming close together. Lifting the wagon flap a little to see out. Watching the other wagons come closer. Watching them slow down. Stop.

"Where are you from?" their leader asked, sliding off his horse.

He was a short man, with heavy arms. A strong face with bushy eyebrows, but he was a man who had more blood in him than white blood.

He didn't wait for an answer.

"I'm Mr. Adams," he said, holding out his hand to shake with Salmon. "Mr. Augustus Adams. You can just call me Double A for short."

"I'm Mr. Brown," Salmon said. "Mr. Salmon Brown. From the east."

They shook hands.

"Where are you from?" Salmon asked.

"We're from Indiana," Mr. Adams said. "We get the winds, the free winds from Illinois and blessings from the great Abraham Lincoln, if you know what I mean."

"Are you abolitionists?" Salmon asked.

"Proudly so, I would say, for as long as I can remember and then some."

"Then maybe you've heard of my father, John Brown?"

"Osawatomie Brown?"

Salmon nodded.

"Well, the good Lord does work in mysterious ways. Not in a month of Sundays did I ever think I would be talking to a son of John Brown." He called to his wife, "Woman, these aren't strangers. These are the kin of Osawatomie Brown." And turning back to Salmon he continued, "I'm good at shoeing and playing the fiddle and if there is anything I can do for you, me or my people—we are at your service."

"We're going to California..." Salmon began.

"My friend, that doesn't come as a surprise," Mr. Adams said. "And so are we, but the way things are, sometimes the traveling news is good and sometimes the traveling news is not good. And the way things are, the surprise might just come in the getting there."

"Good or bad, surprise or no surprise, California is where we are going and we will get there as soon as anyone—sooner than most."

"But two heads are better than one, don't you think? And ten wagons are better than three. I mean there are Sioux Indians around here. So why don't you join us?"

"Where are you stopping for the night?" Salmon asked.

"We were hoping to get to Emigrant Pass, but we can camp here if that is your plan."

Coming out of the wagons. The women and children. One woman coming toward us. A little taller than Mr. Adams. A little darker.

"I am Shirley Adams," she said, almost bowing.

Joining. Once again traveling with a wagon train. Feeling safe. One night. Two. Three. Passing Independence Rock and Devil's Gate. The road turning to sand. The mosquitoes as large as bees and buzzing just as loud.

And then another wagon train. A larger one. Rumbling toward us. Closer. Coming closer.

"How many wagons would you say?" Salmon asked.

Mr. Adams rubbed his chin.

"A lot," he said. "Looks like a lot of wagons."

"Yes, a lot," Salmon agreed. "And I'm thinking it would be prudent..."

"If we joined them?" Mr. Adams interrupted. "I agree because Indians are Indians and we are crawling through their land like snakes."

Watching. Waiting for the wagon train to reach us. And then slow down and stop.

"I'm Mr. Daniels. Mr. Adam Daniels," the leader of the wagon train said.

"Adam? Now that's a coincidence right there," Mr. Adams said. "Do you want to shake the hand of another Adam? Mr. Augustus Adams?"

Mr. Daniels shuffled his feet as if he would walk away.

"I'm Mr. Daniels, from the south, the old south, the real old south..." he said to Salmon.

Salmon hesitated.

"And heading west?" he asked.

"I'm from the south, the old south, the deep south," Mr. Daniels repeated.

"We're no trouble and we'll keep to ourselves..."

Salmon took a deep breath.

"Can we join your train?" he asked.

"A nigger in my train..." Mr. Daniels began.

"We've come this far and we can fight and we could make it on our own but we have women and children..." Mr. Adams said.

"No trouble and we're only asking for a few days, until we get through Indian land," Salmon said.

Mr. Daniels shifted his feet again and swept his arms along the horizon.

"Indian land is a long ways," he said, "clear through the Black Hills to California."

"I have two men who are good with guns," Salmon said.

"And I have six," Mr. Adams added.

Mr. Daniels shook his finger at them.

"Alright," he said, "but we won't be stopping for you. If a woman is in her time or a baby gets lost or a wheel gets loose or an animal dies, you are on your own."

"Only for Indians," Salmon said. "We understand that."

Returning to their wagons.

"They are rebels. They are southern born and bred, dyed-in-the-wool rebels. Can you believe we are traveling with rebels?" Salmon asked and answered himself. "I can't believe we are traveling with rebels."

"Strange things do happen," I said. "But there could be

another way of seeing it, because if we are traveling with rebels, they are traveling with Negroes and Abolitionists and God."

The next night, the sky so heavy with clouds. Then lightning and thunder. Then the rain. Sheets of rain. And hail. Worrying all night. Trying to sleep and keep warm. Hoping not to sink and get stuck in the sand. And then the morning, gray and misty. Walking behind the wagons to make them lighter.

And as we walked, the sun. Warm and bright. Glistening. That is what I remember—the glistening. The sun glistening on the back of the wagon, on the grass, on our shoes. Pleasant, even good to be walking until the glistening behind us turned into something else. It turned into the hard shine of metal. The glistening turned into guns and lances. The glistening turned into Indians—hundreds of Indians in the distance.

Mr. Daniels rode down the length of the train.

"We've been spotted," he said.

"Should we circle?" Salmon asked. "Get the women and children in the middle?" "No, not yet. It's too soon," Mr. Adams said, "circling has to be saved for the positive end, the absolute, very last thing because if we circle before they do anything, they could think that we want to fight. And if we want to fight, they will want to fight. No doubt about it."

Mr. Daniels frowned and tightened his mouth.

"Well, maybe so," he finally said. "Maybe they will think a hundred wagons are too much for them to take on. And we can always circle further on down the road."

He wiped the sweat from his forehead.

"Have you done any killing?" he asked.

Salmon didn't answer. Mr. Adams didn't answer.

"Never mind, as long as your men and your guns are ready."

"Yes, if it comes to anything, we are ready," Salmon said.

"My people are also ready," Mr. Adams said. "And my Shirley is a sharpshooter."

"Good..." Mr. Daniels began, then tilted his head to a side to better hear something.

Listening.

I heard it too.

"Wolves? Could it be wolves?" I asked, thinking of Dianthe, thinking of Zena—and her baby, if it was true that she ever had a baby.

"They're wolves alright, but not the animal kind. That's the howl of an Indian scout. It's their signal."

"Do you know what it means?" Salmon asked.

Mr. Daniels shook his head.

"We might have to circle sooner than we think. But we'll go on for a little ways. Straight away, as fast as we can."

We hurried to get in the wagons. Climbing up the sideboard. Abbie handing Minnie to Salmon. Johanna right behind her, but slipping and falling down under the wagon before Abbie could catch her. Salmon jumping from the wagon to get Johanna. Abbie climbing up to keep the oxen from moving while I was holding their muzzles, praying and talking softly to them, "Just stay. You like to stand and stay. Just do that."

Other wagons passing us. Our oxen raising their heads. Looking. Switching their tails. Bessie stamping her foot.

Annie and Sarah were in our wagon, holding it still. Minnie started to cry and looked as if she might topple down. Ellen climbing up to steady her.

George herding the sheep. One, confused and frightened. Straying. Wandering away. Ezra going after it.

And then the noise. Shrill cries, like a hundred women going through their time. And then the opposite, like something coming and crashing.

Salmon climbed into the wagon with Johanna. Ellen and I hurried to our wagon.

And then it was quiet. Indians riding their horses in and around the wagons. Saying nothing. Doing nothing. Just riding and looking—at the men, at the women, at the wagons, at the animals.

Getting to our wagon. Ellen in front of me, her foot on the wheel tongue, pulling up on the brackets of the jockey box. Annie leaning over to give her a hand.

And then there was another hand, coming up from behind us, an arm, coming up over my shoulder, reaching out, coming between Ellen and me, grabbing at Ellen, grabbing her hair, pulling her back.

"Let go. Let her go," I screamed. Feeling a horse tight against me, pressing me to the wagon. Feeling the Indian riding the horse. His leg. His hand. The smell of him. The paint. I could smell the paint.

"Let go. Let go," I screamed again, pushing against him, trying to twist his arm back. "You can't do it. I won't let you do it. Let my girl go."

And as I was screaming and kicking and pushing, Ellen suddenly turned. I thought she was falling and reached out to catch her. But she wasn't falling. She just lowered her head and lunged forward, her mouth open–and she bit the Indian's hand. Was he laughing? Yes, even though I never thought of Indians as laughing. He was laughing because I remember his mouth. Open, and so big with thin lips and large white teeth.

All the wagons stopped. Men came out with their rifles.

Mr. Adams left his wagon. Slowly, he walked his horse to one of the Indians who was away from the others. On the side. Watching. Red paint splotched here and there on him and on his horse. Carrying a lance decorated with blue and white beads and an eagle feather. Eagle feathers also in his hair, and between the ears of his horse and at the horse's tail.

For a moment, man to man, horse to horse. Then Mr. Adams threw his leg over his horse and dismounted. He dropped the reins over the horse's head and let them go. Slowly turning around, he turned away from the Indian and began walking, one sure and steady step after the other. Walking back to his wagon.

Everyone watching. No one moving. And then Mr. Daniels gave the sign to move forward.

"Don't look back," he said.

The men climbing into their wagons.

The wagons starting to move. Salmon's wagon moving. Our wagon moving.

Trying not to look back. Once again, trying not to look back.

CHAPTER 33

SHE WAS CRYING.

"Mama. Mama. Mama."

Ellen looked at me.

"Don't listen," I said. "Cover your ears."

"Are we turning away?" she asked.

"She is not calling for us and we need to finish this mending," I said.

Crying again. Crying out.

"Oh, God. Oh my God, help me. It's been so long. Too long. It's been so hard. Too hard. Mama help me. Someone help me."

Ellen dropped the apron she was hemming.

"Is that the way it is?" she asked.

"Yes," I said. "That's the way it is."

Still looking at me. Maybe she was wanting me to say more. But what could I tell her? What did I remember? What did I want her to know?

A prayer. "The Lord is my shepherd..." The words lost in moans.

"Are you going to go?" Ellen asked.

Remembering...

The crying. The contractions. The crying. The contractions.

Remembering...

Trying to hold onto something. Trying to hold onto someone. Trying to see past myself, to the window, to the sky. To God.

"A woman needs her own people..." I began.

Remembering...

"It's like dying," my mother said. "It's the closest you come to dying and the closest you come to being alone."

Remembering...

The pushing and waiting for the next push. Knowing the next push would come. Wanting it to come. And afraid. Thinking that there was just a little difference, just a little space between living and dying. Praying that I would be strong enough. Praying that God's light would shine...

Once again, words lost in the crying out. In the sobs. In the moans.

"You are right," I said. "I will go. And if I can help, I will help."

Remembering...

The babies. All the babies. But, no, that's not right because I didn't remember all the babies. I wanted to remember them but they slipped away from me. One baby becoming another. One time becoming another. Remembering that there were babies. Their crying. Their sucking. Their growing...

"Yes, I will go," I repeated.

Walking out between the wagons. Feeling tired. My legs. My head. My back. Stumbling on a stone. Seeing Mr. Daniels. Was he waiting for me? It seemed that way. Standing there, to the side of his wagon, getting ready to boil pots of water.

"It's her first baby," he said as soon as I was close enough to hear him. "Mrs. Lundy has given her a dose of calomel and a cup of blackberry root tea. And I've gone for the doctor, but she won't have him." He hesitated, flames from the fire dancing around him, throwing long shadows against the wagon. "Mrs. Brown, can I ask you a question?" He shifted his weight from foot to foot. "Did you ever have doctors?"

"Doctors? Yes, there were doctors when they could come. I remember three or four doctors. Also midwives. Many midwives and sometimes neighbors."

"A big family..." he began.

"A big family? I suppose to, but I don't know... I don't know about counting children. Children aren't numbers. And anyway, big is up to the Lord, isn't it?"

He waited.

I went on. "Well, it's true, I had many babies and I had them in many places. But I always had my babies, each one, in a bed, in a house. I never had a baby in a wagon train—with the heat and the cold, and the bugs and the dirt. And the Indians."

"We thought we would get to California before..."

Another sharp scream. Mr. Daniels hit one hand against the other.

"Maybe you can help. She's in there," he said, pointing to a high roofed tent.

Opening the flap. Waiting to get used to the dark. Finding Beatrice Daniels in the dark, tossing from side to side, pulling on her comforter, unraveling it row by row.

"Mama. Mama, is it you? Have you come?" she called out.

"I'm Mrs. Brown," I said, sitting beside her. "I am Salmon Brown's mother. And I am the mother of Annie and Sarah and Ellen."

She calmed down.

"Yes, I know Ellen. She was so brave when the Indians came. And that's what frightened my baby. Those terrible Indians. That's when he started pushing..."

I helped her to sit up. Folded the comforter. Straightened the sheets, turned the pillow. I held her shoulders and rubbed her back.

"You will be brave, too," I said.

She pointed to a neat stack of blankets and sweaters and a christening dress. "Before we left, my Mama gave me those clothes for the baby," she said. "And she promised as soon as we get to California, she would send more. Can you tell, Mrs. Brown, do you think it is a girl or a boy?"

I put my arms around her waist and rubbed her stomach.

"It hardly makes a difference," I said. "A girl baby is as good as a boy baby. And soon it will be over. And once it is over, it is over. Finished. Done with. Almost forgotten."

She doubled forward and hid her face in her hands.

"But how can I be a mother when I am so weak? How can I be a mother when I am like a baby myself. A baby giving birth to a baby..."

"Every woman is a baby when the time comes," I said. "Ever since Eve, it's been that way. But every woman finds the strength when she needs it and you will be a fine mother."

I dipped a cloth in cool water and wiped her forehead, her face, her hands, her arms. I opened her blouse, slipped her breast straps down. Sliding the cloth down her back, gently across her chest, beneath her breasts. Thinking she was settling into a rhythm, but then her body tightened and she cried out again, "Mama. Mama. Mama."

Mr. Daniels came to the door.

"I'm going for the doctor," he said.

Beatrice didn't answer. She turned away from the tent opening. She took my hand.

"Is it alright, Mrs. Brown?" she asked with the voice of a little girl asking for a favor. "Is it alright for a doctor to come? He will want to pick up my petticoats and peek at my body, won't he? He will want to touch me all over. His hands—he will creep up my legs."

"All that touching? I remember feeling safe more than touching," I said, wiping the tears on her cheeks. "And looking? Doctors don't really look. And if they do, it's not the same kind of looking and it doesn't matter. What matters is just coming through it all, you and your baby, and then the next day and the next day."

She started to shiver. I held her against me. We rocked back and forth. Back and forth. In a few minutes the doctor came. He lit the lantern. Once again Beatrice hid her face in her hands.

"No complications. Soon it will be over. Breathe deeply," he said, fixing the sheet over her legs and her belly.

Mrs. Lundy returning.

"One more push and I will write to your mother with the good news this very night," she said.

"Beatrice, do you hear me? Can you feel your strength coming on?" I asked. "The baby is almost here, can you feel it?" Holding her hand. Her fingers squeezing into mine. Scratching.

"I can feel it. I can feel it. I can feel my baby coming," she said, half crying, half laughing.

And then, "It's a boy. A fine boy. Small but big enough," the doctor said, slapping it and giving it to Mrs. Lundy to clean.

"A fine boy," I repeated, kissing Beatrice on her cheek, standing up, stamping on my legs to uncramp them.

Leaving the tent. The cool air sweeping down under a heaven of twinkling stars. Holding my shawl against my shoulders.

"I don't know how to thank you," Mr. Daniels said, as I started to walk back to my wagon. He lowered his head, looking at his boots. He lowered his voice. "But I do know how to thank you, Mrs. Brown, because I know who you are. We all know who you are. And some of the men feel deep and wrathful about the family of John Brown. One of our fellows had his brother killed in Kansas..."

So there it was. Kansas. That chilling word. It would always be a chilling word. I could see my family there. In their little houses. Sometimes sick. Sometimes cold and hungry.

Kansas? It was a fight. It was a battle and what happened there, happened there. Did Mr. Daniels think I would say that my family was wrong? Did he think I would say that my family was vengeful and bad?

"Mr. Daniels," I said, "I know about killing in Kansas. My son was also killed there. In the morning, when he went to the barn to feed the horses and milk the cow."

Still looking at his boots.

"And the war. Too many good men dying to keep what was theirs."

"Good men?" I said, starting to raise my voice. "I know about good men. I know a lot about good men. My husband was a good man, my sons were good men..."

"Mrs. Brown, please, don't be angry. Listen to what I am trying to say," he continued, "what I am trying to do is to give you a warning. I want you to know that you and your family and friends are in danger. Do you understand?"

"What kind of danger?" I asked.

"Danger. You are in danger," he repeated.

"Yes, Mr. Daniels," I said. "I do understand."

Walking. Some lanterns still flickering. Some campfires still glowing. Coming first to Mr. Adams' wagon.

"I have been told that we are in danger," I said as we met.

"I am not surprised. Rebels are rebels—probably for life. It's in their bones. It's in their blood."

Shirley Adams joining us.

"Danger? What should we do? Does Mr. Brown know?" she asked.

"Mr. Daniels just said..."

"Danger," she repeated. "I don't think we should fool with danger. Are you going to speak with Mr. Brown, Double A?"

Mr. Adams nodded and picked up his hat.

"And you're right. We're not going to fool with danger. No way. No how."

Walking together, past one wagon. Past two wagons. Mr. Adams stopping. Looking around. Looking at me. Looking at shadows.

"They could be watching us right now, fingering their pistols and watching us," he said. "And black and white walking together might make them see red, blood red..."

Shirley Adams stopped walking and turned to her husband.

"She cried all night. That's how afraid she was. All night. That's what Honey did. She knew they were slavers."

"Slavers... Yes, slavers and trouble, and what I'm thinking, Mrs. Brown, is that you should go on ahead and Shirley and I will follow. Of course, thinking that it's no difference to you," he added.

"It's no difference to me," I started to say, the words not going very far, just hanging there without a finish because suddenly there was a difference. It was a difference I could feel springing up inside me. Churning my stomach. Thumping in my head. It was the feeling of strangeness and heaviness—and anger. It was the feeling as if I was coming to a fight. Feeling as if I could meet that fight. As if I could face it. "Mr. Adams, I am not a man, but I can get angry too," I said. "And I am not going to turn my back on my husband or my sons—or myself for that matter. And I will not turn away from the Negro or from God and His justice and love. So we will walk together."

The anger giving me long steps. Letting me take longer steps. Matching my steps to Mr. Adams' steps.

"Whatever you say, Mrs. Brown," he said.

Coming to my wagon. Ellen sitting up on the front seat.

"I've been waiting," she said. "I couldn't sleep."

"Try again," I said. "Take the feather pillow."

"The baby?" she asked.

"The baby is a boy and he is fine," I said.

Walking to Salmon's wagon.

"There is trouble," I said, reaching for Salmon's hand and climbing up on the jockey box. "They know who we are."

"Who knows and who told you?" Salmon asked.

"All those men," Mr. Adams said. "All those guns. When they come after us, we will be sitting ducks at the first, and dead as doornail ducks at the last."

We closed the flap behind us.

"I knew it," Salmon said. "I knew we would have trouble. It was just a matter of time. Trusting rebels, trusting slavery scum is the same as trusting a snake in the grass. But if they want a fight, they'll get a fight."

"Salmon, they have a hundred wagons. How can we fight a hundred wagons?" Abbie asked.

"We can fight the way we always did, with guns and with the Lord's blessing. Besides," Salmon said, "who is to say there would be a hundred wagons against us? They are not all southerners. They are not all rebels. They are not all murderers. Some of them must be honorable men."

"And supposing there were only ninety wagons or eighty or seventy..." Mr. Adams began.

Salmon cleared his throat. "Mr. Adams," he said, almost sternly, as if he was scolding Johanna, "Not my father, not my brothers, not me—Browns don't turn tail and run."

"Running away?" I spoke quickly, my words coming right up to the end of his. "Running away? Who knows what that is? It sounds bad, but maybe it isn't. And if you run away, you can come back. Isn't there a right time and a wrong time?"

Abbie put her hand on Salmon's shoulder.

"Harper's Ferry—do you remember what you said about going there? Do you remember what you said about fighting there?" she asked. "You said it was a trap."

Salmon's cheeks reddened and he started to raise his voice.

"Do you remember what I said about Kansas? Do you remember what I said about the war? And we are right and we have a right and we have a cause."

"Shush," I said. "They will hear us."

Mr. Adams was fidgeting with the brim of his hat.

"Mr. Brown, my wagons are going to pull out," he said. "As soon as we can."

"Now?" Salmon asked. "Right now?"

He shook his head.

"Now is as good a time as any because it's no secret, but you may not know that my Shirley has it in her mind to live long enough to be a grandma one day."

"Right now?" Salmon asked again.

"Right now. Before she gets shot at. Before Honey gets hurt. Before..."

Mr. Adams put on his hat.

"We will be rolling out. Right now, before they fix that tire that fell off, before they graze their stock and before they know that we know and before they can hitch up and chase us."

He waited for Salmon to agree.

"We can do it," Abbie said slowly and surely. "We should do it. This is not running away from anything," she added more urgently. "This is just going forward, just not going backward."

"Abbie, this is not Harper's Ferry..." Salmon began.

"Maybe so and maybe no," Mr. Adams said. "But black folks know when the time has come to go..." He smiled. "It's a little tune I made up."

He opened the flap and turned to his wife.

"Let's go, grandma," he said.

Climbing down from Salmon's wagon. Walking to their wagon. Slowly. Arm in arm. Their heads high.

Watching them leave.

"They're thinking of their children," I said.
Salmon turning to me. Looking at me.
"Grandma," he said. "Grandma Brown..."
"Then we will go?" I asked.
"Yes," he said. "We will go."

CHAPTER 34

GEORGE DROVE OUR WAGON. Annie went to help Ezra with the sheep in the other wagon. Sarah and Ellen went to help Abbie with Johanna and Minnie. I was sitting up front with George. Peering into the night, trying to see the trail. Trying to see the rocks before we went over them, the trees before we smashed into them, the mud before we sank into it.

Traveling all night. Following the trail as best we could under a cloudy sky. The ruts. The stones. The thorn bushes that could reach past an animal's shoe.

Thinking of Mr. Daniels. Thinking of Kansas. Thinking of John...

"We lived like animals and they hunted us like animals. But we are men in God's image, with God's message on our lips and we will prevail."

A bad man? Did that sound like a bad man? And how could rebels, looking with the blind eyes of Satan, see John?

Coming to a hill.

"Too late to go around it," George said.

Climbing.

Everything that was not tied down or hooked up, starting to swing and bump and bang. Rolling from side to side. The stove tearing a hole in the flour bag. Feathers from the pillow flurrying on the stove. Flour sprinkling the Bibles and boots. The twine and awl and buckskin strings tight against the back wall.

And then a pause. Almost a hush—the short stopping that comes before going downhill, when the swinging and bumping and banging will start again. George shouting, "Whoa. Whoa," and shouting something more I couldn't quite hear.

Going fast. Holding onto the wagon rails. The bumping shoving my stomach into my chest, my head turning from side to side. Going too fast.

"Too fast," I called out. "George we are going too fast. We have to..."

Suddenly there was a jolt and a tilt and the wagon teetered and toppled and just went over, like a person, their knees giving out. Almost a gentle sinking down—and the going and the pulling and the banging—and the fleeing—settled into a stillness and a quietness.

I crawled out of the wagon.

"Are you hurt?" Annie asked.

"Rest awhile," Sarah said. "It's best if you don't move too soon or too quickly."

"What's too soon? What's too quickly? My skin is following after my bones, that's all, and nothing is broken," I said, straightening my dress, brushing back my hair and retying it.

Ellen crawled into the wagon.

"I should have fixed the stove better," she said.

"Looks like everything should have been fixed better, but it wasn't the mess that tipped the wagon," Salmon said, more sad or worried than angry. "Two hours," he continued, "that's what we have until sunup. Then we will be able to right the wagon and go on."

Two hours...

We tidied the wagon. Boiled a kettle of water for tea. Ate a meal of hardtack. Annie showing Johanna how to play a clapping game.

Clap hands... clap hands... till daddy comes home...

Abbie changing Minnie's baby cloth, using the ligament oil to smooth her. Mr. Adams bowing his fiddle and starting to play that song about John. John Brown's body... Liking it and not liking it both—and there were some times when I was hearing it that I could see John, standing tall and straight, his arms behind is back, his eyes twinkling, his mouth resting into a smile. Shirley Adams about to sing, but stopping. Looking at me, then looking at her husband, shaking a finger at him, saying, "No." Mr.

Adams playing the Battle Hymn of the Republic and Amazing Grace instead. Ellen and Sarah and Shirley humming along.

Two hours—the sun rising the color of butter, the wagon righted, the oxen hitched, and the going starting again.

Two hours—and the race was on again.

Terribly hot days blowing hot wind and dust and sand so it was hard to breathe and hard to see and everything was covered with dust and dirt. And terribly cold nights, when we wore gloves and hats to bed and rolled the children in so many blankets they could hardly move. And that one day when the weather changed so quickly, from hot to cold and from rain to hailstones that were as big as a quail's egg.

Fleeing. No longer traveling, but fleeing. Fleeing, as John said, like animals...

Through the snow covered Wind River Mountains, where the trail turned steep and narrow and rocky. Across the Green River, the water sloshing up under the wagons, carrying off buckets and pans. Racing through Wyoming and into Idaho. The rivers. The Sweetwater River. The Snake River.

Whenever we stopped, Johanna asking, "Fishing? Fishing?"

Abbie saying, "Tomorrow. Tomorrow."

Passing the Ice Slough, coming to the Subletter Cutoff, the cutoff to Fort Bridger and the Mormon Trail to Salt Lake City. Taking a moment to stop. To look around. The cutoff almost kind, wide and worn—and easy. Looking at the note posted there.

The Lord shall give thee rest from thy sorrow, and from thy fear.

Mr. Adams reading the note once and then twice. Rubbing his chin. Rubbing his hands together.

"Salt Lake City..." he began. "I've heard tell that's where a man can live with more than one wife."

"A black man?" Salmon asked.

Mr. Adams shook his head.

"Makes no difference to this black man. From the beginning my Shirley has always been enough for me, but the truth is we are tired, sorely tired, with time running out on us. Time running out the backdoor while we are whistling on the porch."

"Whistling?" Salmon asked.

"That just means a shorter trail is as good as any and this shortcut is giving me a nod and a winking eye."

"And I've heard tell that the trail to Hell is even shorter, but we are not going there," Salmon said. "We are going to California. Remember California?"

"Except for the good Lord, there's no one to say we have to be going anywhere, is there? And if it turns out that we are not suited in Salt Lake City, we can always go on later, can't we?"

"This is a free country and free men make free decisions," Salmon said, "but the Browns are not suited to Salt Lake City and we are doing our going on now—to Soda Springs, to the Humboldt River, and all the way to California."

Mr. Adams looked around, waved his arms above his head, as if there was something to catch.

"Whistling, winking and freedom," he said. "Strange bedfellows, as they say, but we die for them and we live for them and sometimes we leave our friends for them."

He reached for Salmon's hand.

"Mr. Salmon Brown. John Brown's son..." he said as they shook hands. "And Mary Brown's son," he said, shaking my hand. "Write us when you get to California. We might just get that old winking sign again."

Saying goodbye. Calling out from wagon to wagon.

"Goodbye. Goodbye."

Calling quickly, so we wouldn't lose time, but still able to watch the wagons turn away to the south. Feeling a lonesomeness. Everyone trying to keep their tempers. Everyone trying to keep their spirits and their hopes.

"Think what it will be like in California," I said. "Just think... A real house. A real garden. Real streets. In a real town—with a school and a church and stores. And our neighbors will listen when we tell them about snow, so much snow..."

"And we will tell them about icicles. And ice—how cold and hard and slippery it is," Ellen said. "And blizzards. We will tell them about the time Joseph got caught in a blizzard and would have died if we didn't find him."

"But we did find him and he didn't die," Annie said. "And we will find our way to California. I know we will. It couldn't be that we have come so far for nothing. It couldn't be..."

And then Sarah interrupting. Drawing in her breath, catching her breath and almost whispering. "There," was all she said. "There," she said again, cupping her eyes and pointing behind us to the east.

Following Sarah's finger. Looking behind us to the east. Looking as far as we could. Looking to the slope of the foothills, to where we were just a few hours ago—and there, like ghosts against the horizon, we saw the rebel train.

Shouting to Salmon.

"They are on our trail. They are on our trail."

Stopping. Three wagons stopping. Three little wagons—like the beginning of a children's story. "Once upon a time there were three little wagons trying to get to California..."

"They are on our trail, but they can't be traveling much faster than we are," Salmon was saying. "If we keep going at a good speed we should make Soda Springs in four, maybe five days and we will be safe there."

"And if they catch us?" Ellen asked. "What will they do to us?"

"Catch us? Who's to say they will catch us? Who's to say what the Lord knows? And we're not exactly ambling and slow-poking along, are we?" I said,

Looking at Ellen. Looking closely. Looking past her frown. Looking past her tight blouse and short sleeves. Seeing how she was changing, seeing how she was coming into her womanly shape and knowing when we got to California, she would need new clothes. Annie and Sarah too. Wondering what kind of cloth I could get. Wondering how expensive it was. Knowing they would need shoes first. Knowing we would all need shoes.

"If they catch us," Ellen continued. She made a face, opened her mouth and showed her teeth. "If they come close and want to trouble us, I'll bite them. That's what I'll do. I'll bite any of them and all of them. Just see if I don't. I bit an Indian and I can bite a rebel."

"When the time comes, we will know what to do, and it

won"t be biting," I said. "That is, if the time comes—and if is a very big word. If is as big as going to California. If is as big as getting there."

Time stretching again. Every day so long now—and always the wagons, like demons, behind us. Following us. Chasing us. Sometimes thinking they were getting closer. Sometimes thinking they were farther away. Sleeping even less. Stopping, when we did stop, more for the animals than for the people. Trying to be patient. Trying to be cheerful.

"It's a known fact around these parts that if the rebels don't get you, the rattlesnakes will..." Ezra began.

"Rattlesnakes? Those cute, coiling, rattling things? That's what I want—a nice hot rattlesnake stew when we get to Soda Springs. Mrs. Brown, you do know how to cook rattlesnake, don't you?" George asked.

"I have a better idea," Abbie said. "We can hang the snakes from a tree and let them slither down on the snakes that are following us."

"Snakes to snakes," Annie agreed. "Let them fight it out."

She laughed. They laughed.

Saying, "Mama, it's funny. You can laugh too."

"In Soda Springs. I'll laugh when we are in Soda Springs," I said.

"Promise?"

"I promise."

Soda Springs...

Saying Soda Springs as often as I said, Dear God, our Father. Please dear God... Saying Soda Springs every time I closed my eyes and saw the graves of my children and the graves of my grandchildren—not back east, but here, in the wilderness, behind that stone, in that ditch, against the sagebrush or the prickly pear. Inside my head. Always inside my head. Blinking. Trying to lose the image. Daytime. Or nighttime. The dream, the vision, the fear... Johanna running to me. Calling to me, "Grandma. Grandma." Shot down as she was running. Trying to get up. Tears turned to mud as I picked her up. Her arms around my neck. Minnie screaming her baby wail. Ellen flapping her arms, trying to fly away—the long sleeves of her new dress floating around her. The others stretched out, blown down into the ground. Sticks in the ground. The ground moving, moving them into a circle and then into a star. Johanna almost still in my arms but holding on. And no place to go. No place to hide. Each step bringing us closer to a grave on this side or a grave on that side. A garden of graves...

Soda Springs.

Saying Soda Springs when I saw the buzzards circling. Saying Soda Springs when I heard the wolves howling.

Trying to pray instead.

Yea, though I walk through the valley of the shadow of death...

And another voice. Hearing another voice. Dianthe's voice. The echo of Dianthe's voice. *Yea, though I walk through the valley of the shadow of death...*

Then our wagon coming over a rise. Coming to a shimmering distance, as if the earth was waving to us. As if the earth was waving us on. Welcoming us. And as the rain clouds were clearing and as the sun was slipping through them, it was there.

"It looks like a castle," Ellen said.

"It might not be a castle for everyone," Annie said, " but it will be a castle for us."

"A castle that's a fort with soldiers," Sarah said, "and when those fire blowing dragon rebels try to get us, that will be the end of them."

Ellen was smiling.

"It's not that I wanted to bite anyone..." she began."

"I know," Annie said, "all that blood and besides you might have gotten broken a tooth."

"And then you would look like a witch. A young witch with beautiful hair," Sarah added. Chattering.

I did not tell them to stop the chattering and the foolishness. "Soda Springs," that is what I was saying, as if I was saying Heaven or home or the Promised Land of Milk and Honey.

The soldiers riding to meet us. Their uniforms as blue as the blue in the flag they carried. The Captain coming to Salmon first. Talking to him. Then greeting me.

"Mrs. Brown," he said, "it is an honor to be of assistance to you and to your family and a rare pleasure indeed to dispel the rumor that you were all murdered in Missouri."

"Murdered, no. But chased, yes," I said, almost breathlessly. "Captain, we have been chased and we are still being chased..."

He nodded. A young man. Medals shining on his chest.

"There is no need for worry, Mrs. Brown,"—and looking at Annie and Sarah and Ellen—"and Misses Browns," he added. "I can assure you that the chase is over."

Following the soldiers to town.

Young men. So young. Too young to have been at Harper's Ferry. Hoping they were too young to have been at Harper's Ferry. Too young to have sprung at John with a sword, to bring the hilt down on John's head, again and again, until John was still and almost dead. Too young... "If I practiced, I could be a horsewoman and ride a horse like that," Ellen was saying.

"They are fine looking," Annie said.

"The men or the horses?" Sarah asked.

"Well, I guess both..."

CHAPTER 35

GREEN.

What else is there to say? Passing mountain after mountain, thinking this is all there is, thinking this is all there will be—another mountain to climb up... Another mountain to climb down... Another mountain waiting to be a trap... Another mountain waiting to be a tragedy...

What else is there to say? Turning another bend, straightening your back once again, lifting your head slowly, looking over the rumps of the oxen and then, when you are expecting to see another shadow and another, you suddenly see green...

What else is there to say when the wagons stop rolling and rumbling and the oxen lower their heads to graze and you look down past your feet—and your prayers—and everyone is pointing and shouting and shouting and pointing...

What else is there to say? When everyone is afraid to hope, or afraid to hope too much. When everyone is older and tired, but not too tired to go on...

Green.

"Everything in the Garden of Eden was green and growing," Annie said.

"Just like this valley, don't you think?" Sarah asked. "Just like..." she hesitated. "Just like...what?"

"A promise," Annie said. "Just like a promise between the mountains. A promise like a rainbow. Like a green and growing rainbow."

"And Heaven too," Ellen said, shaking her head up and down. "I know when you get past the blue sky, there will be a green Heaven."

"Paradise? I don't know if it is Paradise," I wrote to Johnny, "but it could be."

"The valley is like a door," I wrote to Ruth. "I see it swinging back and forth. I see it swinging open."

"It is green," I wrote to Jase, "and the earth is soft and the wind is gentle. There is no doubt that peach trees could flourish here."

"The valley is covered with green from end to end," I wrote to Owen. "The smell of the valley is the sweet smell of grass."

"Sometimes I can hear the Lord blessing the greenness, blessing the grass," I wrote to Johnny. "Green for gardens and crops and pastures."

"If only I could, I would send you some green roots and green air," I wrote to Ruth.

"I think you will understand when I tell you that green has a feeling to it, a deep feeling, a little like velvet or the muzzle of a newborn calf," I wrote to Jase.

"I look through a green door. I think I am smiling," I wrote to Owen. "Maybe I will laugh. Maybe I will learn to sing."

"I have come through the green door," I wrote to Johnny. "It is easy to breathe here. Easy to work. Easy to sleep."

"Looking back? I am looking back only a little," I wrote to Ruth. "It is the best I can do because if I could not look back my heart would shrink inside itself. What do you think? Perhaps the good Lord allows a widow to look back..."

"Six months on the road and our journey is coming to an end," I wrote to Jase. "It is almost like coming home."

"We have arrived in Red Bluff," I wrote to Owen. "We have been greeted. We have been welcomed. We have been helped—not because they are sorry for us but because they are grateful."

And time—growing shorter and shorter—was somehow still green.

CHAPTER 36

WE DIDN'T STAY. We said we needed more space. We said we needed more land. We said we needed more sun. But it's also true that I wanted to feel free, to be able to come and go. I didn't want to feel stuck and I didn't want to feel old—or afraid.

"If it's time to move, we'll move," I said to Salmon.

"It's time," he answered.

And then there was Isaac, the Israelite man. Not that we did anything or said anything. Not him or me. Sometimes there was a look. I'm sure of it. And we touched. We had to, touching when I put a plaster to his chest or when I helped him into a clean shirt. Sometimes when I handed him a plate of victuals and sometimes when I took it from him.

"Mary," he said.

That's almost all of what he said. Living alone and not much of a talker.

"Mary" and "thank you"—and "angel." Once he did say that. Even now looking back, I remember he said that, and he reached for my hand and held it. Sitting in the chair by the window.

"It was your wings," he said. "Your wings..."

I should have been surprised because helping out and nursing—it's what I always did. But I wasn't surprised. Instead, I felt like a girl, a silly girl searching for words.

"You're a strong man," I said.

"And you're a strong woman. Yes, a very strong woman."

Looking at each other and then looking away. Looking at

the door.

"I hope your road is easy," he said.

"And I hope your road is easy and your lungs stay clear."

Did he smile? Maybe. Did I smile? Maybe.

"Mary. Mary Brown," he said.

"Yes," I said. "Mary Brown."

So once again we piled into the wagons, once again piling, stacking, stuffing. Moving from Red Bluff to Rohnerville, and then, a few years later, coming down the California coast to Saratoga, to a white cottage on a hillside with a good view and acres to farm.

A good time, I thought, because the war was over. The country was whole. The slaves were free. And people were free, free to think of today and tomorrow.

Looking back, looking back to the black days? Yes, some people were looking that way. Looking so hard that way, they couldn't see anything else.

"The war is fifteen years gone," I said to the man in front of the others, his face as gray as an outcropping of stone.

"The law of the land is the law of the land," Sarah added, "and we bought this land. It is ours and this is where we are going to live."

"Bloody Browns. Killer Browns. Nigger loving Browns," the man shouted. "Go back to where you came from."

"Why are you shouting? What do you know about the Browns?" I asked, looking each man in the eye, first one man and then the next. "The Browns are God-fearing and God-loving, and we will not turn or bend and we will not be chased."

"And if the blind lead the blind, both shall fall into the ditch," Ellen said, standing by my side, opening John's Bible and reading from it.

"Bloody Browns. Killer Browns. Nigger loving Browns," the man shouted again.

The other men listening. Watching. Waiting. Finally turning away with the sunset.

Dreaming that I was climbing, trying to climb, from rock to rock, higher and higher, past thickets and brambles, over fallen logs and rushing creeks, trying to get to the top, to see past the rock, to see the sky, to touch it.

John coming to my dreams, sometimes giving me a hand, helping me to climb. Sometimes asking, "Do you think the sky is more firm than the earth?"

What did I answer? "Perhaps there is more light..." I said.

"Perhaps there is," he agreed.

"Was your husband a fanatic?" the reporter asked.

"No, he was anything but a fanatic," I said.

"Was he insane?"

"No, he was not insane. He was a clear-headed, sober-minded man. His hatred of slavery came from the simple reason that he loved God."

Stones slipping down a mountain, tumbling into dreams. Tumbling into another dream. A dream to see Johnny and Jase and Owen. To see Ruth. To visit the graves–graves scattered across the country like the dark spots of age.

Saving money. Salmon selling a brace of sheep. Friends sending checks and drafts. And then having the money to travel. To go east. To return.

Coming to Chicago.

"This esteemed lady whom we delight to honor," the state attorney said, "will never be a stranger to our hearts."

Men and women waving hats and handkerchiefs. Clapping. Men and women, white and black, in the great hall, sitting and clapping. Standing and clapping. Together. Like waves coming to shore.

Black soldiers coming into the hall, marching down the aisle, saluting. The Reverend Poss saying, "In the name of ten thousand of the colored race in Chicago and six million in the United States. we pay honor to the memory of John Brown."

Looking at the Reverend. Looking at the people. I nodded. Yes, I wanted to say. Yes, it is wonderful and I am grateful, very grateful. And, of course, pay honor to John but in that honor don't forget the black man. Honor the black man too and pass laws to protect him.

John would have said more. Quoting from the Bible, he

would have talked about right and wrong and justice, and his voice would tremble and ring with truth. And echo—the walls would echo.

Yes, I wanted to say, honor John Brown, but he is more than a memory. He is a promise that will not end and a light that grows brighter and reached into dark corners.

Yes... but I was not John Brown. Is that why I had no words? Is that why I moved my lips but had no voice?

Listening. Speeches. One. Two. Three. Songs. A hymn. Everyone singing John Brown's Body.

His truth goes marching on
His truth...

Then leaving the great hall. So many people trying to shake my hand. Giving me flowers. "He fired the hearts of a million boys in blue."

"Yes."

"His name will be woven into history with a gold thread."

"Yes."

"The clank of chains shall offend us no more."

"Yes."

Escorted to my room across the street.

The hotel clerk greeting me and handing me a letter.

"Mrs. Brown, this is for you," he said.

Taking the letter. Putting the letter on the night table. Undressing. Remembering the letter. Turning up the lamp. A letter from Indiana. Did I know anyone in Indiana? A Dr. Johnson in Martinsville, Indiana? Feeling tired. Putting the letter back on the table. Turning down the lamp. Getting into bed. Getting out of bed. Turning up the lamp. Picking up the letter. Opening it...

Lines slithering into words as if they were the left hand of the Devil. Was it the way my hand was shaking? Was it because my eyes were neither opened or closed—stuck and fluttering?

Words jumping out of the paper, out of the flatness. Devils. Words with hot breath and claws...

"Bones. The bones of your son, Watson," the words said.

I sat down. I held the letter to my heart. I lay down. Still holding the letter, crying to it, singing to it, talking to it. My son...

"Mama." I finally said. "Mama, it's my son. It's Watson. And his bones will be laid to rest."

And then, how long was it? A week? No, I think it was four or five days. Standing with Johnny and Jase and Owen. Standing in front of a box. That's all there was. One box in one room a window and a chair.

"I don't know which way I would want it, to be Watson or not to be Watson, but there is no doubt. It is Watson," Johnny said. "I have measured the skull and I am sure."

Jase putting his hand on my shoulder.

"There is no reason for you to be here when the box is opened," he said.

"Watson," Owen said softly and then louder. "Watson," as if he was calling him. As if he was expecting an answer.

Bones... How could anyone know it was Watson? Just bones. And a name tag.

Feeling dizzy. Feeling faint. Sitting down.

"Where is his love?" I wanted to ask. "Where is his courage? Where is his kindness? Where is his hope?"

"His love and his soul are in Heaven," I said.

I stood up.

We all bowed our heads.

Our Father which art in Heaven
Hallowed be Thy name...

"The box that contains the remains of Watson was opened today," I wrote to Salmon. "I am so thankful that God has spared my life to see this time."

"I wish the rest of his brothers and sisters could be here to see it," I wrote to Annie. "There is no doubt of it being one of them."

"His bones were in a medical school and now they are here—and we are here," I wrote to Sarah.

"Everything goes to prove that it is poor Watson, but there is no flesh and there is nothing about the appearance to tell who it is," I wrote to Ellen.

Death and dreams tugging at each other. Pulling each other down. Tumbling. Tumbling together. Tumbling to the foot of the mountain—and rising again.

Bringing Watson, his bones, back to the mountains. Burying him beside John. Watching. Praying. Holding Belle's arm. Holding Ruth's arm. Trembling together. Crying together. Questions and answers together.

"Is it over?"

"It is over."

"Yes?"

"Yes."

"And it is over?"

Saying goodbye. What did John say—until we meet in Heaven? Yes, until then.

For the last time, visiting family and friends. In New York. In Pennsylvania. In Ohio. For the last time, bringing flowers to the graves, the little graves...

Stopping in Kansas. The reception in the Senate chamber. Sitting on the stage in front of a picture of John and on the sides there were cannon balls, pikes and sabers—as plain and expected as if they were wagons and hitches and plows. As if they were his tools. His tools.... Looking at the cannon decorated with satin ribbon.

"I have the honor to present to you the widow of the man who did more than any other to render the name of Kansas immortal," the Governor said.

More speeches. Honors. Judge Adams showing a revolver that was John's. Putting it down and picking up a package. Unwrapping it. Slowly. Carefully.

"This is a piece of the gallows," he said, almost whispering.

Unwrapping another package.

"And this is his cap."

Then the black cornet band played The Star Spangled Banner and John Brown's Body. Voices rising up. Feeling the voices rising up in me too. Feeling one with the voices. And John's voice—I could almost hear it.

The levee afterwards. Greeting everyone. Trying to greet everyone.

"He gave the first blow to strike the shackles from an enslaved race."

"Yes."

"His name is already enrolled with the greatest and brightest in the history of the world."

"Yes."

"He was a martyr. A visionary. A hero."

"Yes."

Going to Osawatomie. To see where the cabins were. Walking the banks of the Pottawatomie, where the fighting was. Seeing the monument to John. Frederick's grave...

Years. How many years?

The year was 1882 and there was a railroad. Taking the railroad I left the rallies and the speeches and the honors. Leaving the graves, I returned to Saratoga. Leaving half of my family. Returning to half of my family. Returning to my life, to the land, to the view across the mountain, to neighbors and friends. Returning to all of my memories. The photographs, the letters, the newspaper stories. Returning to the medal that came from France.

"From the gallows where he was hung has gone forth the cry of universal indignation," Victor Hugo had written.

A gold medal etched with John's face, glinting golden in the sun.

"The sun will never set on Papa," Ellen said.

But for the others there were no medals. Not for Watson. Not for Oliver. Not for Frederick. Not for all manner of men fallen in the war. Not for a whole race of people doomed only by their skin. And not for the men, those Chinese men, who blasted mountains to build a railroad. In the spring, twenty thousand pounds of their bones were found, it was said.

Mothers waiting for coffins.

Mothers waiting for bones.

CHAPTER 37

AT THE END THERE WAS A RAINBOW. My children walking on it, as if it was a road, as if I could follow, as if I should follow. And John was there too. And Dianthe. Singing. We were all singing. Even I would be singing. I would be with my children and we would be singing.

And my sister would be there too.

And Mama. And Papa.

And there would be no wolves...